FROM PRIMEVAL CHAOS TO INFINITE INTELLIGENCE

From Primeval Chaos to Infinite Intelligence

On information as a dimension and on entropy as a field of force

ARIE S. ISSAR
Ben-Gurion University of the Negev
Beer Sheva, Israel

Preface and concluding chapter
ROBERT G. COLODNY
Professor Emeritus
University of Pittsburgh, U.S.A.

Avebury
Aldershot • Brookfield USA • Hong Kong • Singapore • Sydney

Published by
Avebury
Ashgate Publishing Limited
Gower House
Croft Road
Aldershot
Hants GU11 3HR
England

Ashgate Publishing Company
Old Post Road
Brookfield
Vermont 05036
USA

British Library Cataloguing in Publication Data

Issar, Arie S.
From Primeval Chaos to Infinite Intelligence
I. Title II. Colodny, Robert G.
501

ISBN 1 85972 032 3

Library of Congress Catalog Card Number: 95-79584

Typeset by
WordByte
P.O.B. 3102
Beer-Sheva, Israel

Printed in Great Britain by
Biddles Short Run Books, King's Lynn

Contents

Acknowledgments

The support of Professor Emeritus Robert Colodny, from The University of Pittsburgh, PA, is most thankfully acknowledged. He encouraged me, after I sent him the first draft of this book, to prepare it for publication. He also was kind enough to offer his help in editing this book, rephrasing expressions as well as suggesting new ideas. His remarks which I cited in full were marked by (*). At the end, at my request he wrote an extended preface and a concluding chapter which are part of this book. The help of Mrs Margaret Colodny in the editing and printing of his part is also acknowledged. I would like also to thank Mr Ahuvia Malchin the former editor of *"Alpayim"*, A Multidisciplinary Publication for Contemporary Thought and Literature, Am Oved Publishers, Ltd., Tel Aviv, for his encouragement and for publishing of the abridged form of my book in Hebrew, and to Benny Hendel of Israel's Broadcasting Authority, 'Kol Israel', who enabled me to explain my ideas to the Israeli public, on four radio interviews. The enthusiastic response of the readers and listeners, gave me the courage to approach the English speaking public. Thanks are due to Ayala Bat-Shalom Cousteau for telling us the story of the evolution of the musical notes, and to Mrs Sally Alkon and Dorit Elimelech for typing and correcting the manuscript, and last but not least, special thanks are due to my wife Margalit, for her patience and understanding.

Preface

> To every thing there is a purpose and a time to every purpose under the heaven ... A time to rend and a time to sew; a time to keep silence and a time to speak.
>
> Ecclesiastes, III:1,7

> The dogmas of a quiet past are inadequate to the stormy present. The occasion is piled high with difficulty, and we must rise with the occasion. As our case is new, so must we think anew, and act anew.
>
> Abraham Lincoln, Message to Congress, 1862

> Starting with the testimony of Paleolithic art, we see that man has always tried to separate truth from error and meaning from appearance. This fundamental dimension of human consciousness applies both to the scientific inquiry as well as to the human feeling of transcendence, as manifest in religions.
>
> Professor Ilya Progogine in *Cosmos, Bios, Theos*

Our readers will concede that it is always easy to add a brick to the top of a wall that is in the process of construction. It is quite another matter, however, to attempt to rearrange the foundation of a building which is nearly complete. And this is what Issar is trying to do — to rearrange the foundations of our cognitive enterprise. He does so in part by raising the element of information to a cosmic dimension comparable to the familiar dimensions of space and time. Thus there is created a kind of five-dimensional manifold. This manifold, in turn, is embedded in what he calls the field of entropy. Drawing upon the most universal of all the laws of physics, the second law of thermodynamics, he asserts that all processes in the cosmos take place within and against that tendency of all structures to move toward a state of disorder. Creativity in this schema of things is equivalent to creating islands of order in a sea of chaos.

One will also notice how beautifully the idea of the genetic code fits into the idea of information as a cosmic dimension. We can never again consider life, the process of life independently of our understanding of information flows. And in the same way that Shannon and his information theory of the 1920s was concerned with the integrity of messages, so the modern biologist is concerned with the integrity of the message contained in DNA. Suddenly we see the source of ancient scourges of the human organism, namely, the inheritance of genetically modulated diseases, and there opens up the possibility of intervention at the embryological stage to repair the errors in the information flow that is responsible for the integrity of the anatomy and physiology of all living creatures. If any achievement justifies this epoch in calling itself the age of information, it is certainly this.

When I accepted the offer to write a preface I searched for some literary passages that might reflect the scope of the author's intent; this might be summarized as the human trajectory from beast hood to civilization. It was then that I remembered a drama read during my college days — *Prometheus Bound* by Aeschylus. The reader may recall that in Greek mythology the Titan, Prometheus, defying the gods, decided to come to the aid of mankind. For his rebellion, Prometheus was chained for eternity on the rocky face of a mountain, there to be tortured by vultures. In the drama, Prometheus explains his achievement. Thus spoke Prometheus:

> With reason I endowed them and with mind;
> And not in their disparagement I speak,
> But of my gifts to memorize the love:
> Who, firstly, seeing, knew not what they saw,
> And hearing did not hear; confusedly passed
> Their life-days, lingeringly, like shapes in dreams,
> Without an aim; and neither sunward homes,
> Brick-woven, nor skill of carpentry, they knew;
> But lived, like small ants shaken with a breath,
> In sunless caves a burrowing buried life:
> Of winter's coming no sure sign had they,
> Nor of the advent of the flowery spring,
> Of fruitful summer none: so fared through each,
> And took no thought, till that the hidden lore
> Of rising stars and setting I unveiled.
> I taught them Number, first of sciences;
> I framed the written symbols into speech,

Art all-recording, mother of the Muse:
I first put harness on dumb patient beasts,
Obedient to the yoke; and, with their bodies
That they might lighten men of heavy toil,
I taught to draw the car and love the rein
Horses, crown of the luxury of wealth.
And who but I invented the white-winged
Sea-roving chariot of the mariner?

Though the language might be archaic, it is clear that twenty-five centuries ago the great Athenian dramatist Aeschylus, in *Prometheus Bound* became the first evolutionist, historian of science, and the first to chart, however poetically, man's progress along the dimension of information. The relevant passages are worthy of reproduction here where they serve as overture to Issar's principal ideas.

Our readers will notice that in his early pages, Issar suggests that his readers might feel that a mere geologist should not venture into the complex realms of metaphysics and theology. I believe that his ill-founded modesty rests upon his perception that most people think of geology as being concerned primarily with rocks and mountains and terrestrial landscapes. Modern geology, however, has become a universal discipline. It connects with cosmology and astrophysics to account for the existence of our planet. It draws from physics the radioactive time clocks that permit the creation of geological and biological and even human history. Even as we write, geologists are feverishly digging into the ice caps of Greenland and Antarctica to search for isotopic evidence of past climate change. They are asked now to determine the probability of earthquakes, the eruption of volcanoes, the rise of sea level, and the function of global warming, etc. In brief, geology poses the entire range of the epistemic and ontological problems of all of the disciplines.

In his own work as a hydrologist, Issar has explored the Fertile Crescent, finding evidence of the climate changes and hydrological cycles that made and unmade the great civilizations of that region.

Later in this volume, in a section entitled 'The Information Dimension in Retrospect', I will sketch in an epistemological framework appropriate for Issar's vision. I will then use it to give a non-traditional account of the emergence of western scientific tradition — through the scientific revolution of the seventeenth century and beyond. I will also give a brief account of the two other great pillars of human culture, art and ethics.

Since most scholars agree that the information age will produce a qualitatively different social structure, we look briefly at some of the possible worlds to come.

For decades, scholars working in diverse disciplines have searched for principles that will permit the unification cosmic, social, and cultural evolution. It is my conviction that Issar's vision points the way to a unitary vision.

As a final note of introduction, I recall that the great mathematical biologist, D'Arcy Wentworth Thompson (1961), in his masterwork *On Growth and Form* when considering some of the difficulties of extracting information from the living world, quoted from the Abbe Galini the following: Science is more destined to study than to know, to search for rather than to find the truth.

Robert G. Colodny
Professor Emeritus
University of Pittsburgh
April 9, 1993

Introduction

> The imagination is one of the highest prerogatives of man. By this faculty he unites former images and ideas, independently of the will, and thus creates brilliant and novel results.
>
> Darwin, 1959, p. 364

Since the early days of the history of man, one finds records on man's speculations about the laws of nature. The first endeavors of man to formulate answers to his questions and explanations to his observations were in the form of mythological stories of creation. In these stories, super-human beings, which man called gods, decided the fate of the world. The laws of nature were the reflection of the will of the gods, themselves being a reflection of the will of man himself, his wishes, vices and fears. Man explained this reflectance by declaring that he was created in the form of the gods. This declaration made life more easy for him; it enabled him to picture his gods mentally as well as visually. He taught this to his children, who did the same when their time came to teach their descendants. The stories were thus transmitted from one generation to the next, blended, each few generations, with stories and explanations to contemporary catastrophes, like floods, earthquakes or eruptions of volcanoes.

Many of the early societies were organized on the basis of families and tribes, their leaders were the patriarchs, warriors and sorcerers. When these people died, their outstanding deeds were added to the saga of their people. The gifts and the provisions put in the graves of these leaders, and the abundant evidence for the worship of the ancestors, show that they were believed to pass into another world, from where they could influence the life of their descendants. Thus, the epics that they were telling, became sanctified as time passed, many of these were recited on special occasions, as part of the rituals in honor of gods and ancestors.

The more ancient the tradition became, the more it became sanctified, until it became the religion of the tribes which shared a common origin. Disbelief was regarded as insurrection to the authority of the ancient and contemporary leaders of the society, and as a danger to its survival. Heresy was punished in the most severe way.

Yet, from time to time, free thinkers endangered their life and questioned ancient beliefs and traditions, suggesting altogether new explanations. One of the first revolutions we know about, was when one of the Hebrews, in the third millennia B.C., denied the existence of many gods, worshipped as idols of various forms, and insisted that there exists only one god, an abstract justice seeking divine authority. Another revolution occurred in the sixth century B.C. among the Hellenes. A group of philosophers started to suggest new explanations to the phenomena of nature, based on their observations and logical deductions. A man by the name of Xenophanes of Colophon argued that man has created his gods according to his own form. He said, "If the Nubians have gods, they are black, if the seals had gods, they would have flippers." The seed from which the entire tree of sociology of knowledge was sown. (*)

The gods, whether abstract or idols, had motives which were beyond the understanding of man. These were mostly the events which did not conform with the basic rule, that once man obeys gods' orders, he will be favored. Most of these events came upon man by accident, by chance, not enabling him to forecast them and thus to prepare himself against them.

One of the first disparities he observed was that between creation and destruction, life and death, order and disorder. He observed this all around him, as well as in his own actions. He saw it in the seasons of the year, in the life and death of his beloved, and in his own creations, whether it was a house he built, or his society. He became aware also of the fact, that while building involves an intellectual effort of organization, and putting things into order, destruction needs mainly physical force, and once a thing is in ruins, it is very difficult to reconstruct it.

He attributed the deeds of destruction to the evil gods, and he visualized a constant war between good and evil. The ancient Egyptians illustrated this war, as the struggle between Horus and Seth. The Babylonians chanted it as the war between Marduk and Tiamat, during the New-Year festival. The Canaanites referred to it as the war between Baal and Moth, and the Persians as the contest between Ahurmazda and Ahriman. In order to win the good will of the good forces and appease the bad ones, man offered sacrifices and chanted rituals. Thus were formed the religions. In some societies, the polytheistic religion was replaced by a faith which divided the rule of the world between two forces, the good and the evil, forecasting the victory of the positive force at the end of the days. Later, when monotheism gained ground, the problem of evil versus good became more complicated, as the force of evil and destruction had to be explained within the dominion of one benevolent creator. The answers to this problem differed according to the level of sophistication, which the different monotheistic societies reached. At the most primitive levels the shadows of pagan evil gods prevailed. They were called the devil, Satan and demonic power. The more sophisticated tried to deal with them in a philosophical and methodological way, calling it theology. They adopted many answers, basically suggested by the philosophers of pagan times, mostly from classical Greece, mixing them with Jewish interpretations of the Bible. The almighty creator was described as the spiritual aspect of nature, symbol of perfect harmony. The evil side of nature, was embodied in man's flesh. It was grasped as a result of the 'primeval sin' a challenge to the believer to overcome. Hell, where all forces of destruction were concentrated, was the punishment to those who failed. Being aware of the danger that probing too deep into these problems may undermine the belief in one prominent force, the religious authorities declared their explanations as dogma. Those who questioned these dogmas, and were not satisfied with the official answer, put their life at stake.

The scholars, the fathers of the scientific revolution, which took place in Europe during the 17th century, avoided dealing with the issue of good and evil by adopting the dualistic world view. The French mathematician and philosopher René Descartes divided the world into spirit and matter. To the questions in the first domain one had to apply theological tools, while for material problems one had to use empirical and mathematical tools. In all what concerned the world of matter the mechanistic laws, formulated by Newton were found to give perfect answers. In this world there had to be a cause to any change. The scientist himself, his will, fears and destiny, were of no concern to scientific research. Science had to be objective. All problems concerning ethics were left to the theologians, ministers of religion, and philosophers of the old school. Science was divided into humanities, which included all spiritual phenomena, or those which could not be measured in an accurate way, and natural sciences, where the canonized rules of accurate empirical research were applicable.

This does not mean that the founding fathers of the scientific revolution were not religious people. On the contrary they were deeply concerned with theological issues. God is inbuilt in Newton's *The Principia*. Descartes first asserted that God preserved the quantity of motion in the universe, in order to conclude the law of conservation of momentum. Leibnitz searched for God's harmony throughout the entire universe. Pascal was not able to bridge between science and theology and abandoned science altogether. (*)

Their avoidance of interfering in theological disputes by the scholars, was also because of their dependence upon the good will of the monarchs and their advisors. The academies, which were formed at that time were patronized by the ruling families. Since this was an age of wars of religion in France, and of struggle of crown and parliament in Great Britain, the scientific community avoided being involved in these struggles, and restricted itself to scientific and technological issues. This was made explicit in the charter of the Royal Society of London, written by Robert Hooke. (*)

From time to time endeavors were made to reunite the sciences. One of these was by the Kantian-Hegelian school of philosophy, influenced by the mechanistic-materialistic world-view of Newtonian physics. It reached its climax in Marx-Engels' dialectic philosophy. This tried to explain all phenomena concerning society, and beyond, in the framework of a materialistic world view. This school of thought, although proclaiming itself to be non-religious, adopted the methods of the religious institutions of the past, and proclaimed its world view to be a dogma. The rise and fall of this philosophy is now the object of study of the historians, who belong, according to the dualistic world view, to the spiritual domain, namely humanities.

In the western world, the positivist school of philosophy expressed the tendency to concentrate on the material aspects of life. An off shoot of this approach, which flourished mainly in the USA, is the behavioristic school in psychology. It concerns an effort to explain all psychological phenomena within the framework of a materialistic-mechanistic doctrine.

As science, in the countries not impeded by dogma progressed, a spontaneous trend of unification developed. This was within the realm of the material-natural sciences. Lines of division between the sciences of physics and chemistry vanished gradually. The same happened between these and the biological sciences.

The closing of the gap between the physical and the biological sciences is expressed not only in their success to open new vista of knowledge but also by the unearthing of new dilemmas. This is a cause of confusion to the scientists, who still adhere to the classical deterministic world view. The principle of a detached, objective, observer, his rational or 'common sense' approach as a scientific criterion, have been questioned by quantum physicists. The role of statistical causality rather than absolute causality, introduced by quantum physicists, have bewildered the most outstanding scientists, among them Albert Einstein.

At the same time, the science of genetics in biology has revealed the role of the randomness of mutations in the hereditary processes. Yet the evolution of the world of life shows a clear teleological principle. How could randomness in the micro biological world lead to the magnificent progressive tree of life? How can randomness in the world of particles-waves allow us to have machines and computers, in daily use, which we can operate in the most deterministic way? Can these paradoxes be answered within the framework of Cartesian philosophy, separating matter from spirit?, or should an attempt be made to develop a new philosophy, in which matter and spirit complement each other? Undoubtedly, most scientists will shy away from such an attempt. They are afraid of blundering into the domain of metaphysics and mysticism. Thus, despite the enormous accomplishments in the various fields of natural sciences, the dualistic approach remains dominant. The world of the modern scientist is divided between his laboratory and his self. Scientific research is still regarded to be an objective art destined to reveal the secrets of matter. It has nothing to do with the scientist as an observer, not to speak of his feelings towards his family, society and faith. All these subjects are still considered to be in the spiritual domain, not to be touched by a 'self' respecting scientist.

Another set of problems the scientist of natural sciences is avoiding are those which are concerned with ethics in human society. These too, are left in the domain of the spirit. But the time approaches, when the natural sciences will have to take a stand also in this subject. Some biologists working in the field of genetics were astonished by the sophistication of the antics of the gene to survive. With the selfishness of the gene it is difficult to explain higher levels of life, unless the gain from cooperation with other genes seems to have more advantages, when survival is the aim. But how does the gene know that it has to survive, in the first place? Secondly, how does it know that cooperation is better for it? Is it just by chance, namely trial and error of the first living molecule? or is it by necessity, which was imprinted already, in the first self-reproducing form of life?

It must be admitted that the division of the world into two domains served science well. The results achieved, since the scientific revolution started, speak for themselves. It protected scientists from diversion into metaphysics, and from wasting time on speculations which have no empirical basis. The question yet rises whether this approach has not served its term, and whether it does not now form a block for a conceptual breakthrough. The reasons for raising this question in the first place are the many question-marks which natural sciences are facing now, and which were discussed briefly in the preceding paragraphs, the other reasons being the questions which are held to belong to the spiritual domain. These are related to order and disorder in nature and in human life, to good and evil in ethics, to beliefs and moral values in private and public life. As was discussed at the beginning of this chapter, these questions agitated humanity since early times, and were not solved up to date.

A few options are at the disposal of the scientist when he is faced with a problem, or a set of problems, which evade solution. In the first place he may admit that the tools of research which are at his disposal are not appropriate to deal with these problems. This was the conventional way, and as we know, it yielded no results. Everyone passed the ball to his colleagues' field. The other way is to decide that the present tools are not good enough. This means that one has to try and develop new tools and methods, in the framework of the existing paradigms. This attitude, in the opinion of the author, is preferable to the first one, but it has its shortcomings. It may happen that all the tools and methods were exhausted, and an altogether new paradigm has to be developed. Not realizing this fact may lead the scientist into a frustrating vicious circle of trial and error. In order to avoid this, another direction is viable. This involves the raising of fundamental questions probing the basic issues of the problems. A question of this character, in our case, may be the following: Is it not possible that the answer to questions in each of the domains is in the gap itself, separating the two? Does not experience teach us that in many cases the solution to certain questions was found by interconnecting disciplines? Does not science try to unify the fields, namely to find a common denominator between the various aspects of reality? Why not try and unify the domains of matter and spirit, while trying to circumvent the pitfalls of metaphysics and mysticism?

The reader may find the last suggestion daring if not adventurous, yet the alternative might be, remaining bogged down in the mire of perplexity. Not willing to succumb to such a situation, the author explored the course of a new interdisciplinary conceptual model, which is going to be introduced in the following chapters.

As a matter of fact, the construction of the model, which will be described in the following chapters, started not in order to answer the above detailed general problems, but had a more limited goal. It started as an effort to explain the evolution of intelligence as well as the form of the hominids, by one system of reference. It was concerned with explaining the fact that since the arrival of man on the stage of prehistory, the geologist uses two types of tools to investigate man's evolution. One tool includes the fossilized, material remains of man. The other tool includes man's artifacts, namely flint tools which show progressive evolution. The detailed steps through which the model passed until it satisfied the demands of the author will be explained in detail in the following chapters. Yet this model by itself, concerned with a limited question, would not have been a good enough reason to write a book about. A paper or even a few papers would have been sufficient to report about the findings. The importance of the model, which the author became aware of at a rather advanced stage of its development, were the general conjectures, verging on the general problems of science discussed above.

Put in a nut shell, the model suggests that without being aware of it, we measure our world with an additional dimension to that of space and time. This dimension is information. It is the additional magnitude (to space and time) which differentiates Homo sapiens from the early hominids, as well as the reader at present from what he was in childhood. The artificial meter to measure this dimension is the computer, which tells us how many bits in its memory were used for a certain text or theory. Before the computer was invented the natural meter was the brain, like the foot and the cubit on the dimension of space, before the meter was introduced, and the age of kings on the dimension of time.

In addition to the new dimension also a new field of force is introduced, and this is the field of force of entropy. This field pulls every composite construction, in space-time and information, to disintegrate. It works like the field of gravity. Thus a set of cards, or a puzzle, arranged nicely on a table, will fall to the floor due the pull of the field of gravity, and get disorganized due to the field of entropy. The way to overcome the pull of both fields is by the investment of energy. Thus a rocket will be able to take off only if enough energy is being invested, while the living organism has to be fed constantly in order not to die and disintegrate.

Evolution of life along the dimension of information is a continuous take-off against the pull of the field of entropy.

In conclusion, this introduction is to forewarn the reader, about the chart of the voyage on which he is invited to embark. In order to encourage him to join the author on this expedition, in search for new answers to ancient perplexities, he is advised to reflect on the following sayings of Albert Einstein (1949):

> To be sure, it is not the fruits of scientific research that elevate a man and enrich his nature, but the urge to understand, the intellectual work, creative or receptive. (P. 7)

1 From pebble tools to computers

> Surely there is a vein for the silver, and a place for gold where they find it. Iron is taken out of the earth, and brass is molten out of the stone .... But where shall wisdom be found? and where is the place of understanding?
>
> Book of Job 28:1, 2, 13

In this chapter I would like to acquaint the reader with the process which brought me, a geologist by profession, to work and develop a philosophical conceptual model. I think that I owe the reader such an explanation, as geology is not considered to be a philosophical science. It is considered to be a 'physical' applied science, namely it involves research and examination of material objects, like rocks and fossils. Also the problems it tries to solve are 'physical' in their essence, like: of what elements is our earth built? How were mountains formed, what causes earthquakes to happen, or dinosaurs to disappear, and what chances are there to find oil, water or gold in a certain region. The theories which the geologists bring forth can be tested either by an experiment, for example, by drilling an exploration well, or through the discovery of new phenomena which confirm or negate the theory; as for example, the finding of dinosaurian remains in Antarctica, which proves the theory of plate tectonics. Seldom is geology considered a science which has to answer questions concerned with the philosophical issues of scientific methodology and thought, not to speak of problems regarded by some to be 'para-scientific', such as the reasons for existence, what is life and what is death? what are ethics? etc.

In the first place I will argue, and later try to prove in a more extended manner, that this conventional impression of geology, namely to be just a material science, is not altogether correct, at least from the historical point of view. Geology has stirred up one of the most renown revolutions in the philosophy of science. It triggered the development of the theory of evolution, which undoubtedly has many philosophical aspects. The great mathematician, Herman Weyl, said in one of his essays that evolution was not only the foundation of biology; it was the foundation of all science. Here he had reference, probably, to the theories of stellar evolution, i.e. the life and death of stars. (*) Erwin Schrödinger (1967), believes our age will be called the age of the evolutionary idea. Geology is one of the main foundations on which Darwin's theory of evolution is based. Charles Darwin had the book *Principles of Geology* by Charles Lyell with him on his voyage on the H.M.S. Beagle (Green, 1961). In this two-volume book, Lyell extends the basic theory of gradual evolution of the surface of the earth, or as it was called, the uniformitarian theory. It included also the gradual change in the forms of life as evidenced by the record of fossils. This theory, as confined to the evolution of the crust of the earth, was first described by the geologist, James Hutton, in his book, *The Theory of the Earth*, published in 1788. The guiding principle of this theory was that the present is the key to the past. In other words, the same processes, which can be observed today, working at the same pace on the earth's crust, were also responsible for forming the face of the earth in the past. This theory, as will be shown later, stretched the dimension of geological time to many millions of years, and thus facilitated adoption of the idea of a gradual evolution. Darwin adopted this theory, as a foundation for his theory of evolution.

After this preliminary attempt to convince the reader that geology and philosophy are not altogether alien intellectual pursuits, I will proceed with the story of my part-time diversion from geology to philosophy.

As a matter of fact, I got acquainted with the philosophical facet of geology only when I was working on my PhD thesis. This research involved certain difficulties due to the special geological structure of the region, namely the central coastal plain of Israel, where I was doing my research. The basic difficulty was due to the fact that I was investigating very young formations. The layers from which this coastal plain is built started to be deposited about 3 million years ago. The rate of evolution of the marine fauna during this span of time was rather small; this meant that the characteristic features of the fossils found, had not changed significantly over the course of time during which the layers were deposited. This deprived the geologist of an important tool usually used to identify the age of the layers. This tool is the different character of the fossils in layers of different age.

The only creatures which did change during this last and short spell of the world's history, were the mammals, and especially the hominids. The fossilized remains of these creatures were, however, difficult to find. Bones deteriorate rather rapidly and only under special conditions are the more resistant parts, like the teeth, preserved. Here prehistory came to my aid. This was in the form of flint tools which early man created. The tools served him either as weapons or for preparing his food and clothes. Usually he used hard flint, which was preserved in good shape, many years after the bones and even teeth of the manufacturer of the tools turned into soil and dust. The use of these tools as guides for understanding the sequence of the layers required a knowledge of prehistory and archeology, which I had to acquire.

Before one starts to identify the age of the flint tools, according to their shapes, one has to decide whether a piece of flint is, indeed, a tool or just a broken piece of rock. This is especially difficult when one looks at the most ancient tools, those produced about a million and a half years ago by a man who roamed the plains of Israel, most probably a relative of the advanced Australopithecus whose remains were found in central east Africa (Leaky, 1960).

When I was first shown these tools, called also 'pebble tools' I asked the same question the reader will undoubtedly ask when he looks at the first time on these pieces of flint, namely: How can one tell that this is a tool and not just a broken pebble from a river bed?

The answer is that the breakage of these tools is systematic and according to a plan. Thus, if one collects hundreds of broken pebbles. from a river bed and compares one to the other, he will find out that the directions of the blows and thus the surfaces of breakage are randomly distributed. On the other hand, when a number of pebble tools from different archaeological sites are examined, one can see that there exists a pattern. Each blow which chipped a splinter off the edge of the pebble was aimed to hit the pebble from an opposite direction, in such a way that a cutting edge with a sinusoidal shape was achieved. This means that the creature striking these blows had a preconceived plan of the cutting edge in his mind. As a matter of fact it started with a need, which produced a plan, which brought a series of actions, which resulted in the production of a tool.

One can visualize this man, whether an advanced Australopithecus or a primitive Homo erectus, who needed a sharp tool to either dig out an edible root or to cut up the carcass of the animal he had trapped. His ancestors undoubtedly used some sharp edged, naturally broken pebbles they found ready in a river bed. (The use of tree branches by apes has been observed, and even birds, like the Egyptian vulture, have been observed using pebbles to drop on eggs they are not able to break open with their beaks.) However, the pebbles that the hominid could collect in the river bed, did not fit exactly his needs. He had to help nature, by striking another blow on the already edged side of a pebble. If the freshly broken pebble still fell short of his needs, he hit it again. By trial and error he slowly learned the best procedure to form the pebble into the shape required for its purpose.

This plan, conceived in the mind of this man, more than a million years ago can be traced by us, while examining the tool and its sinusoidal edge. We can even imagine his grin of satisfaction after the tool was finished, and performed well. This plan, once successful, was passed from the inventor to his colleagues, was copied by other tribes, and was taught to their descendants. We know this because one finds tools of the same design and age, in Africa, Asia and even southern Europe.

Undoubtedly the first steps of prehistoric man were very slow and before the production of the typical pebble tool with the sinusoidal edge, many tools were produced which were given only a few touches by man. In these cases, the archaeologist cannot be certain whether he holds an artificial tool in his hand, or just a broken pebble. In sites where broken pebbles are found beside broken bones and other remains, they are a source of debate between the prehistorians as to whether they are tools or not. Until some special method can be developed to answer this question, these arguments will continue.

When one goes to younger layers of prehistoric times, everyone agrees today that the flaked flints found in layers of soil and clays, are products made by human beings. The pioneers of prehistoric archeology, however, did not find it easy to convince their contemporaries that these stones were produced by a primitive man. One of these pioneers was John Frere, a Fellow of the Royal Society of London, whose account of the flint tools found together with bones of unknown animals was read before the London Society of Antiquaries in 1797. However, more than half a century was to elapse before the idea of the antiquity of man was taken seriously. Today when we look at these tools it is difficult to explain why enlightened people did not deduce that these were tools, once it was shown to them. Here one arrives at the question of the causal relations between the world view of the scientist, and his openness to new observations, not to speak of new interpretations.

The dependence of the awareness to new observations on an

already existing hypotheses was one of the lessons in the philosophy of science, which I learned while investigating the geology of the Coastal Plain. Once the conceptual model of its geology and thus paleo-environments was established, I could go and locate sites most suitable to paleo-mans' dwelling, for example ancient marshes and lakes where man could hunt the animals which came to the water. This enabled the discovery of a site in the coastal plain of Western Galilee. The clay and loam layers at this place contained an abundance of tools and of the Lower Paleolithic period,(Abbevilian culture ca. 500,000 years before present, i.e. B.P.) as well as teeth of elephants, hippos and wild boars (Issar, 1979).

In a site south east of Tel Aviv, where the industrial zone of the town of Holon now stands, the collection of fossils and tools was most impressive. At the bottom of an excavation, in layers of black clay, one could find elephant bones and teeth, together with hand-axes (Evolved Acheulian culture, Mid-Paleolithic), produced about 200,000 years B.P. Flint blades and scrapers, (Mousterian culture-Upper Paleolithic) dating about 80,00 years B.P., were found not far from there. Above them were arrow heads of very refined workmanship, dating about 15,000 years B.P. (Epi-Paleolithic). Nearby, the overlying red loams yielded a collection of shards of beautifully decorated pottery from the Hellenistic and Roman periods of about 2000 years ago. On the surface of the sand dunes, one could find steel balls from shrapnel shells, from the time when the front between the Turkish and British army during First World War extended a few miles to the north, and two-pound anti-tank gun projectiles fired, most probably, during training by the British tank corps during World War II.

The question which occurred to me at that site was whether the evolution of the competence of man, as revealed in the increase in the sophistication of his tools, was the same process which caused the evolution of the form of man from Homo erectus, through Homo neanderthalensis, to Homo sapiens. Another question was whether the evolution of the form of man was due to the same factors which caused the evolution of the animals, for instance the elephants. The next question was more complicated. One could tell a primitive elephant from a more evolved one, according to the form of its bones, tusks and molars. Thus the evolution of the form of the elephants involved the evolution of the form of its body, which included its tools. On the other hand the evolution of man was in two separated entities: in his corporeal form and in the form of his tools. The complex question could then be framed in the following way: Were the processes of evolution which caused the changes in the form of elephants the same as these which caused the corporeal changes of man, and were these processes of evolution also responsible for the changes in the form of the artifacts of man. In other words, the general question which crystallized, stage by stage, was whether there exists a general theory which may explain the evolution of all the remains which were found in the layers, bones, teeth, flint artifacts, pottery and modern artillery remnants.

The first answer which came to my mind was 'complexity', but the question was, how can one measure complexity? Could appearance be the measure of complexity? If so, a contemporary knife, not to speak a rifle bullet, looks less complex than even the pebble tool.

The question of measurement of the level of complexity of tools involved, as a matter of fact, the measurement of complexity of the manufacturing as well as the use of tools, namely the complexity of the behavior of the human being, which is identified with the culture characterized by a certain type of tool, be it a flint or a metal tool.

I will not go into the details of all the questions which had to be answered when dealing with the behavior of living creatures, for example the difference between instinctive and intelligent behavior, as one has to remember that a bee-hive or a bird's nest may also be regarded as a tool, built instinctively. In these questions I was helped by the results of the research carried out by Prof. A. Bitterman (1965), who defined the difference between instinct and intelligence as 'the ability to develop a new way of reaction when an entirely new situation comes up'. This research showed that the evolution of intelligent behavior is a function of the level of the place of the species on the evolutionary scale. Thus a monkey could learn things which a mouse could not. The latter was more intelligent than a dove, which still could learn things that a fish could not. As ascent in the level of intelligence was parallel to the appearance of these forms of life on the geological time table, this meant that the tree of life could be measured also according to the level of intelligence.

The observations on the chimpanzees, carried out by Jane Goodall (1963) showed that they are able to produce very primitive tools, by breaking off a branch from a tree and using it as a weapon. The same could be said in regard to the hominids, namely that the higher is the level of intelligence of the producers, the more complex the tools became. In other words, the evolution in the sophistication of tools is a measure of the evolution of the intelligence of the producer. Granted this, the question remains how to measure the level of complexity, or sophistication of tools?

At that time I came upon the book of the French prehistorian and philosopher, Thailard de Chardin (1965) and found out that he had already described the process of evolution of life as that of a perpetual increase in complexity. Although I arrived at the same general conclusion, I thought that this idea has to be more refined, and better defined, namely that the description of complexity by itself is not sufficient, but one has to find a way to describe organized complexity.

The principle question which thus crystallized at a rather early stage of my inquiries was how to describe the evolution of the organized complexity of tools? As this could be correlated with evolution of intelligence, which could be correlated with the general evolution of the world of life, the general question was how to describe all these modes of evolution by one general theory.

As one looks at the tree of evolution, it is obvious that the evolution of complexity of form can be described graphically, by using space and time coordinates. In other words, change of forms due to evolution, as time advanced, can be described as changes in the geometry of the bodies.

The question which followed was whether the same set of coordinates is good enough to describe evolution of intelligence? As I had to give a negative answer to this, the following question, was whether there exits another single set of coordinates, or a single frame of reference, by which the evolution of form as well as that of intelligence can be described?

This question conceals a certain pitfall, from the conventional scientific point of view. It involves the treatment of the change in the body, which is a material entity, together with the treatment of the change in intelligence which is a spiritual entity. As mentioned, these two entities were declared by one of the fathers of modern science, namely René Descartes, to be separate entities. He taught that the material world should be the realm of study of the natural sciences, while the spiritual phenomena should be investigated by the philosopher or the theologian. This body-mind dualism was adopted by modern science. Since then, it is still the principle paradigm of natural sciences.

The reader may ask here, why did I insist on a general theory, or a single set of coordinates? Why did I not adopt the conventional division between 'material' or 'physical' phenomena, describable on space-time coordinates, and 'spiritual' phenomena, with 'mind' involved, described on another, altogether different and separate coordinate? The answer, is that science strives to give to the maximum number of questions the minimum number of explanations, as science is in a constant search for generalizing theories which will explain a maximum number of observations. Otherwise science would just be a collection of a myriad of laws, each explaining but a few observations.

I knew however, that while striving to arrive at such a generalization, some guidelines have to be taken into consideration. In the first place, the general framework has to obey the laws of logic and mathematics. In the second place, it should not be refuted by observations. These guidelines will still be discussed and debated at length in the following chapters. They are mentioned here, in order to assure the reader that I did not allow myself the luxury of indulgence in mystical theories, but kept myself within the constraints which are intrinsic in scientific methodology. For the time being, it can be said that I view science as a perpetual effort to arrive at the fewest, but most general laws, as possible. These laws should encompass the majority of observations and should be based on logical-mathematical reasoning. The test of the credibility of the laws is their being able to predict and explain new unknown phenomena, and in some instances to suggest experiments which will verify them. Taken to the extreme, we can say that science looks for one law which would encompass and predict all other laws.

Such a wish was expressed by the French physicist Pierre Laplace at the beginning of the 19th century. He mused about an intelligent entity which would know all the forces controlling nature, and at the same time, the momentary conditions of all entities of which nature consists. This entity 'would be able to embrace in a single formula the movements of the largest bodies in the universe, as well as those of the lightest atoms' (Laplace, 1951). He hoped that nothing would be uncertain for this entity; the future and past would be equally present to its eyes. Science has lost many of its aspirations with regard to certainty since Laplace made this speculation; however the wish to generalize is the basic impetus for scientific thought and, as will be discussed later, a basic characteristic of intelligent thought.

Thus, my contemplation as to whether evolution of form and evolution of intelligence can be described within the framework of one system of coordinates was, to my opinion, a legitimate scientific concern, as long as this description is based on empirical data and logical mathematical considerations. In other words I claimed that the quest for one frame of reference or one set of coordinates on which to describe the evolution of form and intelligence is just another step towards generalization, which can also be described as a striving for a holistic theory of science.

At one time I had some hope that the modern science of psychology, especially behaviorist psychology, would provide the bridge between body and mind. I was disappointed at this point, as I found out that this science belongs to the school of thought which still maintains that intelligent behavior of a living being is just a complex mechanical set of acts stimulated by sensory data. As I got better acquainted with the processes of the accumulation of knowledge, as well as the functioning of the brain and the neural system, I came to the conclusion that the mechanistic approach is an over-simplification. It is just an off-shoot from the materialistic-mechanistic philosophy or doctrine, which itself, is a derivative of Newton's physical world view, or paradigm. This states that the world is just a big machine and thus everything, including intelligent behavior, should be explained by the laws of matter and mechanics. If one adheres to the mechanistic approach, one has to be content with the coordinates of space-time, namely the coordinates along which the physical and chemical conceptual models are describable. These are also the coordinates used in designing mechanical robots, when one excludes the software guiding them. As intuitively and experimentally I came to the conclusion that these coordinates are not sufficient to explain intelligence, my search had to continue.

Another school of thought which was dealing with the problem of intelligence, and which I could not accept, was that of the 'vitalists'. The adherents to this doctrine claimed that all efforts to explain life phenomena on the basis of physical-chemical laws are in vain. They believed that the force which causes life is undefinable, and physical-chemical laws can only explain phenomena on the edge of life. Since intelligence is a central issue, they believed it should not even be examined with the ordinary tools of research of physics and chemistry. The most famous exponent of this theory was the French-Jewish philosopher Henri Bergson (1974). The splitting of the world into two was in discordance with my principle of searching for an holistic approach.

The school of philosophy, which conformed to my search for one general framework of reference, was that of 'organism', based on 'system theory'. The main exponent of this school is Ludwig Von Bertalanfy (1968). This school maintains that life is a function of its being an organized system. Characteristics of organization, whether of a living organism or a society, are concepts like those of wholeness, growth, differentiation, etc. Such notions do not appear in conventional physics. In other words, there is no linear progress from the individual parts to the complex organism, once parts are functioning together as an organism, they follow other laws than those governing the behavior of each part as an individual. The laws of the whole organism are the laws of life.

As the reader will see, the conceptual model which will be developed in the forthcoming chapters is in some ways an 'organismic' model, yet the answers suggested by the system theory did not answer the basic questions, which I have posed above, namely: whether there exists a general frame of reference or a dimensional entity, in addition to space-time, in which the evolution of complexity and organization of form, of behavior, as well as intelligence can be described?

2 The dimension of information

> I am convinced that even much more is asserted: the concepts which arise in our thought and in our linguistic expressions are all — when viewed logically — the free creations of thought which cannot inductively be gained from sense experiences.
>
> Einstein, 1949, p. 22

In order to find out whether an additional subtle dimension exists, and what might be its character, the first question I asked myself was: what is that which differentiates a primitive flint tool from a more evolved one? I also asked the question: What more do I need, given the materials, to produce the more sophisticated tool than the simple tool. The answer which came to my mind was more knowledge, or more information.

I then asked myself what is the meaning of knowledge and of information? What is this that turns an event we have observed, or a word we have heard, to a mental picture? This led me to books dealing with the mind and the processes of understanding. At last I came to the conclusion that there exist two main streams of thought regarding this problem: one which believes that all the work of the mind will be understood in a physical-chemical context once a better understanding of how the brain works is achieved; the other which maintained that the mind is a spiritual entity which can never be explained by material science, and has to be treated by psychologists, in the best case. This of course brought me back to the starting point discussed in the preceding chapter.

At this stage it occurred to me to ask the question, whether mind itself and all what it encompasses, like thought, knowledge, information and meaning, does not represent a basic entity of which our world is built. The next stage was to ask myself, whether this entity does not hide an additional dimension, namely, something by which we measure our world.

While I was pondering on this possibility, there came to my hands the proceedings of a symposium on the mind. Brain (1968), one of the participants in this symposium, concluded his presentation with the following words:

> To end with a speculation, I suspect that our difficulties arise in part, at least, from our analysis of events into a four dimensional space-time. We can describe events in this way, indeed we are compelled to do so by our own biological organization, but I fancy that there are living events which we will fail to understand until we can describe them also in terms which may involve additional coordinates. Then we may transcend both the old materialism and the old mechanism.

These words, coming from an expert in the field of the works of the brain and mind, encouraged me to proceed with my endeavors to understand what 'understanding' really means.

Most readers will find it tiresome to have the detailed description of how I finally came to the conclusion that, indeed the entity, which we call mind, thought, etc. does entail a new basic dimension. The readers who are interested in this process, are invited to consult my publications referred to in bibliography (Issar, 1980, 1982, 1984)

Before the subject of the new dimension I came upon is discussed, one should not forget contemporary tools, namely the computer. For many scientists, among them geologists, computers are the main tool of work. As a matter of fact, it is difficult to find any occupation in a modern society which is not connected in some way with computers.

It is difficult for us to imagine these computers being replaced by another tool, as undoubtedly it was difficult for Stone Age man to imagine his tools being replaced by others. This is due to the simple reason that if we, or he, could have known of something better, then the more advanced tool would have replaced the old one. Yet we can assume that a few hundred years from today, the computer will be the tool of the past (the same as the mechanical calculating machines, so popular not more than two decades ago). One can imagine a museum of technology some hundreds of years from today presenting an exhibition of personal tools. It is quite probable that the stone tool (ST) will be included, as will the personal computer (PC).

The reader, however, does not have to wait until the computers, as obsolete tools, are exhibited in the museum of technology in order to realize that it is more complicated to produce a computer than to produce an abacus, and it is more complicated to produce these tools than a flint tool. To the question, how can this complication be quantified, it can be suggested to use the same computer as a meter. For this purpose, one will have to prepare a computerized algorithm or flow-chart of the instructions to produce the tool. These instructions can be given in the form of words, or illustrations, or mathematical symbols. In all cases the algorithm for the production of the metal and electronic tools will be longer than that for the flint tools. The reason is that, while that of the flint tool involve just the collection of the material, the preparation of metal needs the processing of the material by fire, and the computer needs electricity. In principle however, the instruction charts can be based one on the other, for example, the group of instructions to collect materials can be presented on the monitor of the computer by one symbol, or code-sign, either word, picture or symbol. Thus from the point of view of length, or number of bits, the instruction chart of the modern tool may look shorter. But once we want to explain it to a more primitive society, these code words have to be deciphered, namely explained by extension.

Granted that such algorithms or instruction flow-charts have been prepared in an extended form, and loaded on our PC, the reader should ask himself: what does the value showing the number of bits loaded in the memory of his computer, for each set of activities, mean? It is suggested that one define this new entity as information. It differs also in a loaded computer from a one that has just been switched on. It is claimed that this is a dimensional entity, like space and time. Thus instead of saying more information is needed to produce a knife than a flint tool, one has to say: the knife is higher on the dimension of information than the flint tool; likewise the computer is higher than the abacus. The same can be said, of course, about the inventors of these tools.

In order to help the reader digest this new approach to information, it is suggested that the reader asks himself: what is the difference between himself when he was a child and himself at the present state while he reads this book? He has grown up in size, namely expanded along the three directions of the dimension of space. The time passed, or in other words he advanced on the dimension of time, but at the same time he acquired knowledge, which is based on information. This was accumulated and stored in his brain in a certain order. We have thus two processes: the first involves the turning of sense data into brain data, which can be explained by chemical-physical processes of the functioning of the brain (like the work of a camera) while the other process is the translation of this data, into knowledge. For example, one and one, either sheep or wolf, make two, in other words, to generalize and arrive at the logical laws of mathematics and cause and effect of individual, particular episodes. When the reader, does this, or any other process of assemblage and interpretation of knowledge, he grows, or expands, not in spatio-temporal terms, but along another dimension. It involves the process of abstraction of space-time events and their accumulation as data, or notions. This dimension, it is suggested, to be called information.

It is important to clarify that information and knowledge are not synonyms. Information should be considered a construct by the mind operating on raw, unclassified data. Knowledge is defined as the union of a number of sets of ordered information. (*)

It should be immediately added that thought involves not only the abstraction of events, namely turning events into notions, but its putting into order, that is, information-about-information, or the change of information according to information. This act is described as a movement in the field of order-entropy, again with analogy to space-time relations which can be described as a field of gravity. This will be discussed in detail in the following chapter.

In order to try and convince the reader that information is a basic dimension, like space and time, and already in daily use, but not recognized as such, it is suggested to discuss the experiment of the process of hatching of eggs in an insulated incubator. Let us ask what are the differences between an egg, a chick and a hen. The differences are, undoubted, measurable along the dimension of time, (still grasped by us as, 'time passed' instead of movement along the dimension of time) and along the dimension of space, which is expressed in the changes in size and form of the bodies involved i.e. from yolk to chicken. Such a change can be described on a space-time coordinate system. Yet the changes in space time were directed by a code, which first of all differentiated between a fertilized to a non fertilized egg, and later produced a certain chicken, and not a swam. To this code biologist will refer as information. But when asked what makes a hen wiser than a chicken, one will answer that it has more experience, namely it acquired more information from the environment and processed it. Once the quantitative term 'more' is used, it means that something was measured. What exactly was measured? To help the reader answer this question he should ask himself what does the value showing the number of bits loaded in the memory of his computer mean? As will be discussed, it is suggested to relate to the additional quantitative entity which differs a hen from a chick, as well as a loaded computer from a new one, just switched on, as information. It is claimed that this is a dimensional entity, like space and time. Thus instead of saying the chick has grown during the period of the experiment and acquired more information, one has to say, "It progressed along space-time-information dimensions" (the same as did the observer who investigates the behavior of the chick).

The author will not be surprised, if the reader will not readily agree to regard information as a dimension. The author knows, how important it is for the ego of everyone, himself included, to regard thought, as his personal talent. One would encounter the same difficulty when he will try to explain to a Japanese wrestler, that his weight, he was so careful to cultivate, is just space-time curvature.

For the time being, until the grasping of information as a dimension is accepted, the reader should consider the possibility that there exists such an additional dimension as some kind of a mental exercise — namely, to try and see his increase in wisdom with the years, as movement along the dimension of information.

The plea to the reader to take this dimension seriously, namely, as more than a mental exercise, will involve reminding him of the fact that the advancement of science is not different from the evolution of the knowledge of the individual man. It involves a process of the gradual emancipation from the anthropocentric mindset. This can also be described as a shift from an entirely subjective to a more objective understanding of the world. Thus one may expect a psychological barrier, a function of his anthropocentric, subjective, pre-convictions when he gets involved in the search for an altogether new conceptual frame of reference or dimension. These sentences are written as a warning as well as a challenge to the reader who is ready to proceed with the further steps of the development of a new conceptual model.

In our particular case, the question is whether the process of objectification for grasping the dimensions of the world around us has already been accomplished, and whether our world view is detached from of the subjective folly of the childhood of mankind. This may manifest itself in man's maintaining that general phenomena are a function of his personal activity. As I argue that indeed this is the case, I will present now additional arguments in order to convince the reader that, indeed, the process of learning or collection of information is not his own subjective activity, but a movement along an objective dimension of information.

For grasping better this possibility, one can assume that when asking a child, or one of our ancestors from prehistorical times, what is space and time? He would have answered, "All which is around me, and which passes when I do something, or when I live." Sure enough, it would not have occurred to him that space and time are objective entities or dimensions characterizing the world on the whole, which includes among other things the observer. The same question now is posed to ourselves, namely is it not possible that we do not merely collect information, but that we move along a dimension of information?

I will try now to substantiate this suggestion, namely to regard information, similar to space-time, as a dimensional entity along which an observer moves when an event of observation takes place, by asking first of all, what is a dimension?

We know that we refer to all events and objects in a quantitative way. Thus we may refer to area, heat, hardness and velocity in a dimensional attitude. Physics teaches us that some of these dimensions can be reduced to more basic ones. For instance, heat can be described in the terms of the velocity of molecules. Yet, there exist still a few basic dimensions which cannot be reduced. The most basic dimensions are space-time. It is regarded as a four-dimensional continuum, the reason for this being that space can be measured in three directions (x, y, z), while time is one-directional (t). Every point on these four-dimensional coordinate systems can be described by four numbers (x, y, z, t). Every such point (when it is space-time it is referred to as a space-time event) has an indefinite number of neighboring points.

For the purpose of distinctness of meaning, it is suggested to refer to space and time as dimensions, while to x, y, z as directions. It can thus be said that space is a dimension with three possible directions (or in order to locate a point in space one needs three values in three directions) and time is a dimension with one direction. An event in space-time can thus be described by quantifying the directions from a certain point of reference. A point-instant event will be that in which the extension of the body on space-time coordinates is at its smallest value, described as space-time without a direction. Once it has one direction it will be a line, two directions a plane, and three a volume. The same regarding time, which when devoid of direction will be referred to as an instant (having no past and no future). The present is an instant. Thus a space-time event, without direction, will be termed a point-instant event.

Let us assume now a number of point-instant events, located randomly around us (twinkling stars may be a good illustration) and a conscious observer counting them. Instinctively the reader will agree to this suggestion, namely that the observer counts the space-time events. In other words, the act of observing and counting is attributed to the observer, although on a second thought it will be agreed that the events as well as their number, may exist even without an observer doing the act of counting. Here comes the question whether this way of description of the event is not done in a subjective way, namely whether the way we describe the observation which is going through a process of being counted is like saying I counted seconds, instead of saying I moved along the dimension of time along the length of 20 seconds.

This question needs undoubtedly an additional clarification, it may be rephrased in the following manner: Is it not possible that due to our anthropocentric attitude we regard the information about the events around us as something which starts from us, rather than something which is an intrinsic part of the event itself

The next question will be, what is the directionless entity on the dimension of information, which is analogical to the 'point' on that of space and 'instant' on that of time. It is suggested to regard the 'notion' as such a directionless entity. This will mean that the directionless event in our world is the 'point-instant-notion-event' event, or the PINE.

The question which has to be answered now, is how does one measure on this dimension? To answer this question the act of measurements of space and time have to be investigated in more detail.

As mentioned earlier, measurement of space is done by a spatial meter which is a sequence of points, and time is measured by a clock which counts, or moves along the sequence of instants. A question which will be postponed for a while is that of the continuous and infinite versus the finite of each dimension separately: the question which will be dealt with now is the continuity between the three dimensions. It is relatively easy to explain that space and time are a continuum, even in a non-mathematical way, as it is obvious that any measurement of space involves the passage from at least one point to another and this needs time. Its measurements requires a spatial clock. Or in other words one cannot grasp the passage of one instance of time to the other, without imaging a movement from one point to the other; and as space is a continuum, and time is a continuum, than space-time must also be such. When one considers information, and asks oneself how it is related to space-time; one should take into consideration that its measurement involves the act of counting or adding one point-instant event to another. As it is argued that the act of counting is not more, not less than movement along the dimension of information, it can be claimed that this dimension is intrinsic in space-time. In other words the reader is requested to realize that counting is not the act of the observer but of the observed event, namely the fact that space-time-information is a continuum, and thus the movement in it involves counting.

In more general terms it can be said that the dimension of information makes space-time measurable. As a matter of fact, it can be said that information makes space-time finite, or turns it into point-instant-notion events or PINEs.

The understanding of the act of measurement of space-time in connection with the dimension of information, and the claim that counting is not an attribute of the observer but of the observed, enables a further step in the understanding of the dimension of information. As was suggested, the measurability of our world, is a hidden dimension intrinsic in the space-time-information continuum. This means that if the dimension of information is abstracted from space-time the movement on this dimension is by counting, namely, addition, i.e. induction and deduction. Thus, the dimension of information is two-directional.

Explaining induction and deduction as movement along the dimension of information, helps to get out of the vicious circle created by David Hume's argument; that all efforts to guarantee the certainty of the inductive results are themselves inductive in form. The getting out is similar in some aspects to Kant's suggestion of innate categories; but instead of categories it is hereby suggested to speak of basic dimensions; and each inductional step is a step on the dimension of information. Thus one cannot guarantee the certainty of inductive results without a meter of induction which is induction itself, as one cannot guarantee the certainty of travel in space without travelling with a spatial meter.

The question immediately following is whether induction and deduction are possible without involving the dimension of information. For example, measurement space is the addition or the induction of space units. The answer is that there exists a difference between space as an entity which is just space, and metric space, which is also observed space, namely the statement about the intrinsic nature of space-information.

Before the interdependence between the space-time-information (STI) dimensions is further discussed, the question of units of measurement has to be clarified.

The meter, the foot, the year, the month and day are some of the conventional units with which the world is measured. It is beyond the scope of this book to tell the story of the evolution of the calendar and the technics of the measurement of space and time. Since the scientific revolution of the seventeenth century the scientists made an effort to define objective units of space and time. Today these units are measured on the atomic level. Yet with all the objectivity and precision of the measurements of space and time, there still remains a certain degree of conventional assumptions. For example when an astronomer measures the distance of a certain star with his radio-telescope, and reports the distance in a certain figure of light-years, he assumes that the velocity of light through space is constant, in space and time, namely that the photons of light which reached his telescope, after leaving their source many millions of years ago did not have to obey other laws of physics than these formulated on earth at present times. The conventional time scale for geologists is the year, and the distance of geological eras and ages on the dimension of time are measured by millions of years. There are two clocks used by the geologist to measure the age of rocks. The first is the relative clock which is decided by the presence of fossils and the sequence of geological events. While using this clock the geologist assumes that the length of the year, as decided by the velocity of the movement of the earth around the sun, and the number of days in a year, as decided by the velocity of the rotation of earth around itself, did not differ significantly in the past from that of the present. The absolute age of rocks is measured by the decay of radioactive atoms. This is done by measuring the ratio between the original radioactive substance and its products, derived by radioactive decay, found in the rocks. This clock is not influenced by the astronomical year which is the time needed for Earth to travel around the sun. While using this clock, the geologist assumes that the physical law by which he calculates the rate of radioactive decay did not change. The two assumptions, put together, say that if the dinosaurs would have used a calendar and a clock, their time was not different than ours, not to speak of the calendar and clock of Australopithecus, roaming the plains of Tanzania. Also at present, one assumes that during all the time he performs a certain measurement, space-time does not change. This assumption is important, as the theory of relativity tells us that time and space are interdependent and are a function of the relative velocity of the observer and the observed. In other words, the space-time scales are not absolute, but for events measured and occurring in velocities well below that of light, the change in space-time is neglected. On the other hand, if one happens to travel in a rocket which is accelerating and which approaches the velocity of light, he is told to be very careful when he compares the results of his measurements with that of his colleagues who did not join him for this trip.

Physicists are positive that the change in space-time while approaching the velocity of light is a reality. They also assure us that there exists no observable velocity greater than that of light. On the other hand, one of the basic assumptions of the physicists is that the logic of the mathematical calculations carried out by the observer do not change even when the rocket carrying him approaches the velocity of light.

If one is ready to assume that information is a dimension, like space-time, one might ask the question whether it is not possible that this dimension also is going through a change, when an observer is approaching the velocity of light This question may be phrased in the following way: Is it not possible that instead of saying that information about space-time changes when one approaches the velocity of light, one should say space-time-information relations change at this velocity. In other words, it is claimed that the physicists, while they were sure that what they do is just to observe their clocks and meters, in reality their observation was a set of PINEs, due to the subtle dimension of information, intrinsic in the world.

The reader will undoubtedly raise the question of how it is that the physicists, among whom one finds people who reached the most astonishing intellectual and material accomplishments in the history of mankind did not notice the dimension of information.

The answers to this question involve, in the first place, the already expressed claim about the still prevailing anthropocentric approach to the world of most people, among them the physicists. In the second place it involves the paradigm, in the framework of which the various physical theories have been formed. This paradigm maintains that only repeatable observations are to be considered when a physical theory is proposed. This involves the measurability of the physical parameters like space, time, mass, energy, etc. by conventional and calibrated instruments, like meters, clocks, balances, thermometers, etc. Physicists are careful not to go beyond these parameters which will get them involved with phenomena which their instruments are not built to measure. Another basic assumption of the current paradigm of physics is that there is an agreement, but no interference, between the laws of mathematical logic and the physical world. This separation between the works of matter and the works of mind is a function, as a matter of fact, of the problem faced by the pioneers of physics and mathematics, like Descartes and Newton. They had to reconcile their 'natural philosophy' and their religious doctrine. This brought them to divide matter and spirit. This, to their opinion, also ensured an objective, non biased approach to the physical world and its processes. This approach, which will be discussed later, was challenged already by some quantum physicists, like Wolfgang Pauli (Laurikainen, 1989). Last but not least, it is claimed that in some domains of physics, like thermodynamics and quantum mechanics, the dimension of information is taken into account, only that it is regarded as the probability factor, which, as will be discussed in the forthcoming chapters, is a function of the quantity of information in the system of observer and observed phenomena.

Let us return to the suggestion to consider the logic of our mathematical way of thought as a dimension which may change, at the velocity of light, in a similar way to which space-time changes. Let us assume that the basic unit of measurement on this dimension is 1+1=2, and let us assume that we send again the rocket with the space-time measuring robot connected to a computer which calculates the velocity of the rocket, and other vehicles which he observes while accelerating. What we know is that during the time that our rocket is below the velocity of light, the velocities of the vehicles passing in the opposite direction to that of the observing rocket can be added to that of the observer to give the relative velocity of passage. But the second the rocket reaches the velocity of light, these velocities cannot be added anymore.

The physicists will say that there is no observable velocity beyond that of light. Is it not possible to say that 1+1 is not any more 2, beyond the velocity of light? In other words that the dimension of information has shrunk like that of space-time and thus 1+1=1.

In order to illustrate these arguments it is suggested that one regard space-time-information dimensions as a three-directional coordinate system (x, y, z). A body expanding spatially will be illustrated as movement on the space direction; the time needed for this will be measured on the respective coordinate. If the unit on the space coordinate will be 300,000 kilometers, and that on the time coordinate, one second, then all the range below the velocity of light will be within that light-cone. For more information about the light cone the reader is referred to Eddington (1959) and Hawking

(1988). This means that anything outside this cone, namely which has super light velocity, cannot be observed physically. To this space-time set of coordinates it is suggested to add the dimension of information. The basic unit, equivalent to the velocity of light in space time, is the logical sentence 1+1=2. The base of the cone becomes thus parabolic, and the meaning of the cone is that anything beyond its envelope, namely beyond the velocity of light per logical sentence is not in the competence of our mathematical logic to comprehend or calculate. This is more or less what is conventionally said about the area outside the light-cone; the only difference is that in the model presented here, the logical-mathematical comprehension is not regarded as an anthropic property but as an intrinsic property of the nature of the world together with space-time.

Examining this light-information-cone, it can be said that its apex, or the locus of the intersection of the space-time-information coordinates, can be referred to as a point-instant-notion event (PINE). It is suggested to call this locus the smallest quantum of observation. The conclusion from this suggestion is that if we go on reducing the size of an event, we will reach a finite PINE at which we will not be able to discriminate between space and time and information. This says that one has to expect a state in which it will be impossible to distinguish between a spatial point, a temporal instant, and an informational notion when dealing with entities approaching the minimum sizes of space-time and information.

What really happens at these extremely small measures, or what are the states of minimum extension, will be discussed later when the conclusions from the present conceptual model will be examined for their more general applicability, other than that from which this model has been constructed. For the time being it is sufficient to say that according to this model, one has to expect logical rules to look different when the velocity of light is approached, as well as when the minimum magnitudes of space-time-dimension are dealt with.

After the question of the unit or the dimension of information has been discussed, we should continue to deal with the question of what is the instrument by which one measures this dimension. The answer was already included while discussing the problem of measurement at velocities approaching the velocity of light. It is suggested that one regards the brain as man's intrinsic part or subjective instrument, by which he measures the dimension of information (like his foot or cubit for measuring space and his pulse for measuring time). As an objective instrument it is suggested we take the computer. Thus, when a scientist or a layman looks at the monitor of his computer and gets the number of bits of memory which he has used and which are still free, he is just looking at a ruler by which he measures some length on the dimension of information.

As a matter of fact the brain and the computer are capable of measuring an additional value and this is the measure of order. This concept will be discussed in the following chapter. For the time being it is sufficient to remind the reader of my suggestion to define order as information arranged according to information.

If the reader would like to review an illustration which demonstrates best, the three dimensionality of our world, he is advised to look at the picture on the cover of the book by Hofstadter *Gödel, Escher, Bach: An Eternal Golden Braid* (1979) and consider Escher, as the portrayal of figurative space, Bach as a symbol of harmony in time, and Gödel, as an exemplary of information. All three dimensions are interconnected in an eternal continuum, and their orderly structure gives us in space the most beautiful paintings and architecture, in time the wonderful pieces of music, and when it is just information about information, the ingenious works of mathematics.

But let us take the pieces of a jigsaw puzzle, of one of Escher's pictures made of thousands of components, and let us throw it into the air to fall on the table? What are the chances that we get the picture in the ordered way as Escher painted it. Let us change the order of the notes of the fugue that Bach wrote, or mix the symbols in the mathematical functions that Gödel suggested. Will it still be Escher, Bach, or Gödel? Why is order such a substantial component of what we consider to be an achievement of mankind, and why do we have to invest energy in order to achieve it?

3 Entropy as a field of force

> What is order? This is a difficult question, and one upon which, so far as I know, nothing at all has been written. All the authors with whom I am acquainted are content to exhibit the genesis of order.
>
> Bertrand Russell, 1937, p. 207

Order is something which intuitively one knows when it exists, but most people will encounter a difficulty when they will be asked to define order.

Analyzing the intuitive observance of an ordered situation, one finds that he will say that things are ordered in space, if he may find, or foretell the position, of one object, after he knows the position of other objects, or how they are arranged. In other words, a system will be recognized as ordered, if one can observe a principle which allows to forecast the distribution of its components. The same can be said about things that happen on the dimension of time. One will say that there is order in time when there exists a periodicity. There is also order in numbers with no relation to space and time, the most simple order is the arithmetic one of 1, 2, 3, 4. More complex sets will form series of numbers which may be very complicated. Yet if one studies a series of numbers once he gets to know the principle or the key for their arrangement, and will be able to predict what should be the next number, he will admit that there is order in the set of numbers.

As was suggested in the preceding chapter, abstract mathematical and logical steps, express movement along the dimension of information. When one considers the order of objects in space and time, he will find that the capability to forecast, depends on the possibility to describe in an abstract or logical-mathematical way the arrangement of the items involved. This means that the principle of forecasting the location of an object along spatial coordinates, or an event in time, involves, by definition, the dimension of information. Thus it is suggested to conclude that one cannot talk about order in space, or in time without the dimension of information, and vice versa, as any prediction needs a spatial brain or computer. This is just another way to say again that space-time-information, should be regarded as a continuum. Thus if one observes a mason constructing a wall, laying the bricks in an ordered pattern, he should be aware of the fact that the order in space that he observes, exists also as an abstract pattern in the mind of the mason, namely arranged along the dimension of information, and it takes time to think, to observe and to construct this order.

The question which was not answered yet is; but what is order? The example of the pattern of bricks may help us to illustrate our definition, which is: Order is information arranged according to information, or: information as a derivative of information. Going back to our example, we will say that the pile of bricks, has minimum information (or is on the lowest point on dimension of information, while its size will describe its position on the dimension of space and mass will describe its position on its space-time dimensions). The most simple pattern of the bricks, for example their arrangement in a line, or a row, can be described as the simplest movement along the dimension of information, namely, 1+1+1..., or a, a, a,.... Their arrangement in a certain pattern, in the line, for example according to their size or color, when each different number or letter pronounces a different characteristic, will be formulated as a, b, a, b.... The set {a, b}, can now be described as a general set A, and thus, when the order in the first row of bricks is described by A, A, the mason knows in what order to lay the individual bricks. The second row can have a more complicated order, namely, a, A, a, A... The pattern will become more complex the more subsets arranged according to more general sets exist.

As mentioned already order may be either in space, in time, in information, as well as along two or three of the dimension together. The performance of a dance by a bee, is an event of order along all three dimensions. Before the discussion of the question of order and disorder, is continued, the evolution of this concept in the scientific thought has to be described.

It is quite surprising to find out that the treatment of the physical aspects of order, was a result of the investigation of the problem of disorder. This was a result of the dealing with a technical term namely 'entropy' for the formulation of the Second Law of Thermodynamics (SLT).

It started at the end of the 18th and continued into the 19th century with the investigations of the father and son Carnot on the efficiency of steam engines and in trying to reach the ideal machine where all heat is converted into motion. This wish was based on the First Law of Thermodynamics (FLT), namely the law of conservation of energy. It stated in general terms that if motion is turned into heat for instance due to friction as is the case of boring bronze cannons, then the quantity of mechanical energy needed for the boring will be equal to the heat energy produced by the friction. Believing that the flow of heat is reversible Sadi Carnot tried to find the conditions in which such a complete cycle is possible. These conditions were found however to be non existent in machines, from which came out the empirical second law of thermodynamics, (SLT), formulated by Lord Kelvin in 1852 that it is impossible to convert heat energy completely into mechanical energy.

In 1865 the physicist Clausius reformulated this empirical principle and introduced the concept of entropy, defining it as the relation between the two states of a heat-work system defined by the ratios of heat to temperature before and after a certain operation. The SLT states that the entropy of an isolated system after the operation, equals or exceeds the entropy before the operation. In other words when heat energy is transformed into kinetic energy the entropy level of the kinetic system will be lower, namely that some energy dissipated during this transfer.

Clausius then generalized the SLT for all the universe, defining it as one tremendous big isolated system, stating that while the amount of energy in the world is constant its entropy is in constant increase, or in other words, that the universe is in a constant shift towards a state of maximum entropy. In more poetic words this means that slowly but surely, the world around us is moving towards its end.

At a certain stage, entropy came to be equalized with disorder. This was done by James Maxwell and Ludwig Boltzman in the second half of the 19th century, by applying the mathematics of probability to the kinetic theory of gases. This enabled them to obtain the average speed of the molecules of air at each level of temperature. This they did by applying the theory of probability, namely by asking what is the most probable velocity which one will get if he catches at random a molecule and measures its velocity. This approach was a daring thing to do, as physics at that time was considered to be a science which deals with deterministic phenomena and which the results of its measurements have to be precise. In the case of the lack of precision the fault was not put on the object being measured, but on the subjective physicist performing the measurement.

Boltzman went a step further and after formulating the SLT and entropy by the mathematics of the theory of probability, he explained this law by combining it with the terms of order and disorder.

Starting from molecules of gas in a container the SLT tells us that the average velocity of the molecules will be higher, the higher is the temperature. If one connects two vessels, one of high and the other of low temperature, the velocity will become the average between the two averages. The question rises why do not the molecules of higher velocity pick up the velocity of molecules in the vessel of the lower velocity and by this increase their velocity? which will result in a higher velocity namely temperature. In other words, why temperatures between two vessels of different temperatures average and not add? Boltzman's explanation is that it is not impossible but it is of very low probability as can be seen from his formulation of the SLT. ($E = -k \log p$, when E = entropy, k = Boltzman's constant, p = probability). Accordingly this law says that the increase in entropy which is equated with disorder is proportional to the logarithmic value of probability, which means that the most probable state is that of high entropy or minimum order.

The SLT, was formulated and subsequently the term entropy was phrased for thermodynamic systems, and indeed many physicists and philosophers of science maintain that this law and term should be restricted to these systems (Denbigh 1989). On the other hand many see it as a universal law applying to all phenomena which involve order (Davies 1988). The hypothesis developed in this book, supports the second generalizing approach to the SLT, it claims that the behavior of thermodynamic systems, according to this law, is just a partial and a special case. In a more general form this law should be applied to all phenomena in the universe, where spontaneous decrease of order or increase of entropy occurs. As will be proposed soon, the reason for the universal drift towards minimum order i.e. maximum entropy, is due to the existence of a universal field of force like that of gravity.

For explaining this proposal let us perform an experiment. Let us take a package of cards and arrange them according to their numbers and series on the table. Let us operate an air blower, which will cause the cards to fall to the floor. What are the chances or probability that they get arranged to give us the same order which they had on the table?

One can do the same experiment by using dice or dominoes, and ask the question what are the chances that they will get arranged according to their numerical value ?

The answer of Boltzman will be by giving a probability value. The higher the number of the cards or the dice the smaller is the probability, of their falling into order, which means that complex ordered systems have a lower chance to exist than simple systems.

Maxwell Boltzman's expression of order (or lowering of entropy) as a case of low probability, has an important impact on the conceptual model of our understanding of nature. It says that the natural trend in any isolated systems will be to reach the highest state of disorder. As a matter of fact Maxwell suggested that to reach a high state of order one has to consider a demon which is in charge on the door between the two vessels and lets only molecules of a certain velocity to pass through the door. As such a demon does not exist, nature cannot divide between slow and quick molecules, black and white which causes them to get mixed.

Coming back to the present hypothesis, and continuing with Maxwell's trend of thought, one will claim that once he observes order, there must be hidden, somewhere, some demon. Thus, if one mixes two types of gases the one heavy and the other light, and let them settle down he will find out that they put themselves into order, in the way that the heavy gas will be concentrated at the bottom of the vessel while the light one on top. Maxwell's demon in this case is the gravity field of earth. The same can be said in regard to the ordered movement of the celestial bodies, which raised man's wonder since he started to raise intelligent questions. The reason given today, for this order, is, that the sun, moon and planets behave in an ordered way in space and time is due to the laws of gravity first expressed by Isaac Newton. The reason that gravity causes the celestial bodies to move in an ordered way is first of all because of the law of inertia formulated by Galileo Galilei. This said that a body will tend to remain in constant movement and constant velocity if no force intervenes. On this Newton added the force of gravity which he imagined as a simple mechanical force. He needed then some kind of a material named ether, in order to transmit this force through space. After all experiments to prove the existence of this material failed, Albert Einstein described gravity in the terms of a field of force, like the field of electromagnetic force, first described by Maxwell to explain the influence between magnets and electricity. A complementary description of the field of gravity suggested by Einstein, was a geometrical one, namely as the curvature of space-time, which says that one can imagine to oneself the field of gravity, as a topographical map, the coordinates of which are space and time and any mass which attracts other bodies forms a topographical sink into which lighter bodies move naturally.

Continuing on with the present hypothesis from this point on, the question is whether one should not look for an additional field of force when one observes a process of decrease or increase of order? The movement towards a more ordered state, opposite to the direction decided by the arrow, dictated by the SLT, will need investment of energy, like in the case of movement against the force of gravity or a magnet.

This question, brings to a more general question: If the SLT expresses a field of force in thermodynamical systems, does not the universal trend, which involves order in all systems, including a package of cards, express a universal field of force? In this case the movement towards a more ordered state, like life, means movement against the pull of this universal field, which demands the investment of energy, again, similar to the movement against the pull of the field of gravity, which also requires the investment of energy.

This question can be phrased also in the following way: Why entropy altogether? Why does science take it as granted that a certain universal process exists and why scientists do not look for a reason behind this? Why is it that when an apple falls from a tree, a force responsible for its fall was looked for, but when it comes to a system getting disordered, scientists take it as granted?

As was mentioned already, the answer to these questions, which is the basic hypothesis in this book, is that indeed, as in the case of gravity, there exists a field of force which causes disorder. In order to convince the reader to consider the existence of such a field, it is suggested to investigate the example discussed in the preceding chapter of a fertile egg inside an incubator, the latter contains a sufficiency of air and was initially raised to a temperature high enough for the hatching of the egg. The incubator was thereafter surrounded by perfect thermal insulation with the consequence that its total entropy can only increase or remain constant. Denbigh (1989) in his defense of the limited meaning of the SLT, argues that if the egg dies 'there is an entropy increase accompanied by the process of disorganization'. The question is: why should entropy increase and why should there be a process of disorganization? To show that this question is legitimate, from the scientific point of view, we will ask also: why is the egg not floating in the mid air of the incubator. The answer, of course, will be that it is known that the incubator, and the egg in it, are influenced by the field of gravity of the earth. We have thus a system and a sub system influenced by a field of force. We know also that if the egg is placed on a shelf in the incubator, it is liable to fall. One will not look for the reason for the fall in the egg itself, but in the pull of the field of gravity. Returning to the first question, concerning entropy and disorganization, it is suggested to consider the possibility that similar to the field of gravity, there exists another field of force which acts perpetually to increase the entropy of the incubator on the whole, and the disorganization of the egg in particular. Only the investment of electrical energy, helps to move against the pull of this field. In more general terms, it is hereby suggested to perform a mental exercise, similar to that which Newton might have performed when he was looking on the apple tree. This exercise requires us to look for a force outside the system, as the reason for its undergoing reduction in order, namely, increase of entropy (whether it is an inanimate or animate system). The same trend of thought will bring us to correlate between the need to invest energy in order to keep, or increase, the order of a system, to the energy, which one has to invest in order to act against the pull of gravity and giving this correlation a geometrical expression, it can be stated that while the field of gravity can be described as curvature of space-time, the field of entropy is curvature of space-time-information.

Physicists, will undoubtedly oppose the suggestion to regard entropic processes, as analogical to gravity or electro-magnetic field forces, arguing that by definition a field of force have to be reversible in time, namely every movement can be reversed to get back to the initial point, and the movement, forward and backward, can be precisely measured. On the other hand thermodynamic systems are by definition irreversible in time, this is connected with the conjecture of the 'arrow of time' which is intrinsic in the theory of thermodynamics. Thus according to the SLT, there is a perpetual loss of order in the universe, and thus each moment, on the dimension of time, differs from its neighbors. Moreover thermodynamical phenomena obey statistical laws, and cannot be precisely measured.

The main answer to these arguments can be by distinguishing the field of entropy as a special field, due to the number and character of the dimensions, along which this field is measured. Conventional physical fields, and as a matter of fact non-quantum physics, are restricted, by definition, to space-time measurements, and do not take the observer, which is the information-meter into consideration. It is claimed that once the observer, and his world view, are introduced into physics, reversibility and precision disappear as shown by quantum physics. The argument, that this will not comply with the universal SLT as expressed by Clausius, i.e. perpetual increase in the entropy of the universe, is answered by the counter argument that Clausius formulation, did not take into consideration nor the amount of galaxial order, nor the amount of ordered information, which is imprinted in the bio-world. As an illustration one can ask the question, how to calculate the energy balance of the system called: Clausius arriving at the SLT. While pondering on this question one should not omit the amount of energy invested in the bio-world, since the first environment-responsive molecule i.e. conscious organism, came into existence. If one insists that still universal order may show a perpetual decrease, the author will ask whether the condition of reversibility is maintained in a gravity field considering the expanding universe theory. In other words does not the expansion of the universe enforces an arrow of time into conventional physics and physicists?

In order to convince the reader that this sort of questions is in the first place, legitimate, and that in the second place, the answer to it may be obstructed by man's anthropocentric attitude, the reader is reminded that expressing the phenomena of electro-magnetism and gravity as fields, he had also to break through a psychological barrier. Einstein's (1962, p. 146) claimed that 'The emancipation of the field concept from the assumption of its association with a mechanical carrier finds a place among the psychologically most interesting events in the development of physical thought'.

As is well known the mathematical expression which describes the free fall of a mass particle in the field of gravity, is Newton's equation:

$$F = G\,Mm/r^2$$

when:

'F' = Force on a mass particle 'm' due to another mass 'M',
'r' = Distance between the masses,
'G' = Newton's universal gravitational constant.

The equation for the field of entropy, if the reader is ready to give this field a psychological chance, was as a matter of fact suggested already by Boltzman-Maxwell's formulation of the Second Law ($E = -k \log p$, when E = entropy, k = Boltzman's constant, p = probability).

At this stage the term probability has to be discussed in a little more detail, but again the scope of the book is not enough specialized, to do the full justice to this subject, the reader is thus referred to Keynes' (1962) book *A Treatise on Probability*. In the following lines I would like to concentrate on the question of probability, in the framework of my general hypothesis and try to convince the reader that 'probability' is equivalent to 'ordered information', which is proportional, according to the Boltzman-Maxwell's formulation of the SLT, to entropy.

There are events which one would classify as improbable, others as probable, and there exist events which will be classified as certain and beyond any doubt. All these definitions refer to events in the future or on the dimension of time ahead of the present. All events which have happened already, and which became past, are excluded from the realm of probability, namely; there is nothing more certain, than something which did happen to us. Yet the more such events are accumulated on the dimension of time in the past, connected in an unambiguous way by a cause and effect ties, the more probable they will seem to us to happen again. The conclusion which looks at first sight as self-evident or even redundant, is that probability is a function of our experience in the past. Such are, for example, the cosmic events which the individual and mankind experience from the first day of their consciousness. In the first place comes the rise and dawn of the sun, events which are classified as certain and beyond any doubt. One can say that the probability of these events is infinite. Thousands of years of experience has taught man to depend on the order of these events and knowing their exact time and place, he could even chart his location upon the globe. Cosmology tells us that the sun will one day disappear after the burning out of all its nuclear fuel but this event is on the time scale of billions of years, thus for the time scale of humanity it is regarded as infinite. Thus although knowledge tells us that the disappearance of the sun is probable, experience gives its appearance an infinite value of probability. One can say thus that a constant record of order is in proportion with probability.

The reaction to this constancy of periodicity was certainty. The organism adapted itself to this certainty by building different types of clocks within itself. We experience these clocks in our daily routine, when we get tired at the end of the day, as well as suffer from a jet lag. Thus one of the tools of evolution was the adaptation to the periodicity dictated by the cosmological events.

The second example to examine the relation between probability and knowledge is a solar eclipses. Such events are frequent and ordered on the historical scale of time, but are not monotonous, and of low frequencies on the life scale of the individual being. The accumulation of experience led the astronomers to build a conceptual space-time model of the solar system and today the recurring of such an event in space and time is predictable as the sunrise. Yet this knowledge is restricted to the men of science, while for people without knowledge such an event will have little probability. Primitive observers, man and animals will even react with panic.

Considering a space-time-information coordinate system, these events can be described as non-monotonous yet periodic waves. We can say that such a periodicity does not reflect itself in instincts, the reason for this is the long duration between one event to the other.

The third geocosmic event will be the fall of meteorites. If we ask an astronomer what is the probability that a meteorite will hit his telescope tomorrow, he may give us a statistical value. He will calculate the frequency of known meteoritic events, their distribution in space, and will produce a certain value. One can say that the temporal and spatial probability of meteorite fall is low and thus its random value is high. This value depends however entirely on the limits, or order of magnitude of precision one wants to arrive at, in space-time magnitudes. If one would like to know what is the probability of a meteorite hitting the globe during a year, the probability value will be rather high, while when one limits the space to the diameter of a telescope and the magnitude of time to the length of a certain day, the value of probability rises in a logarithmic way and will become asymptotic with infinity. We can see also that the living world did not develop any instinct behavior, to deal with the fall of meteorites, while animals are known to react instinctively to earthquakes.

This brings us from the heavens to the depth of the earth. The knowledge of plate tectonics as a scientific theory, gives quite a good background to forecast the probability of earthquakes. The accuracy of the forecast is again a function of the precision requested by the formulation of the question. We call such events stochastic which says that the longer the range or wider the space the more accurate will be our forecasts. In this case of randomness we can see that the living organism did not develop any clock which is tuned to the reoccurrence of the events, when an earthquake happens knowledgeable people as well as primitive creatures will instinctively react with panic.

All these examples enables us to consider the living organism as some kind of an order-probability-meter, the more ordered was the periodicity of an event on the dimension of time, the more ordered information was recorded by the organism, and thus, the higher was the mark of probability given to the event.

Coming back to Boltzman-Maxwell's formulation of the SLT, we can say that if probability is proportional to ordered information, then entropy becomes also proportional to information, but in an opposite direction, namely the higher is the level of ordered information the lower is the entropy of the system. The inverse proportional relation between ordered information and entropy, is as a matter of fact, pronounced by the negative value (–) in the Boltzman-Maxwell's equation for the SLT.

Another understanding of the correlation between entropy and information comes from Information Theory, although the term information used in this theory is not the same as that defined in the preceding chapter. In this theory, developed by Shannon and Weaver (1949), the term 'information' means 'information carrying or storage capacity' of any system of communication, like telegraph, telephone and radio. It was found that the loss in the intelligibility of messages sent through such systems of communication, are due to many factors which can be described altogether by one symptom, termed 'noise'. The increasing distortion of the messages, in relation to the original form in which the messages were sent, (not particularly to their meaning, from the point of view of their intelligent context) by 'noise' was found to be analogous to the dissipation of heat from a hot vessel into the surrounding. This dissipation, as was mentioned, is according to the SLT. Thus if for example a message containing many words is transmitted, each word with a different frequency in the message, (namely its probability of appearance is different), then the total information regarding this message carried through by the system, is the sum of contribution of each word, (in a logarithmic value, due to its probability of repetition) multiplied by its probability. Shannon's equation of information is analogical to Boltzman-Maxwell's formulation of the SLT. The main difference is that in the later, the constant k is an absolute value, while in the Information Theory k changes according to the different system and message. Yet, one cannot avoid the general conclusion, that the loss of meaning of a certain message, either just an arrangement of numbers, or a chapter from the Bible, is through a process similar to that which determines the increase of entropy in a thermodynamic system. This means that Boltzman-Maxwell's formulation of the SLT, is a general equation of any process in which the distinctiveness of any system from its environment, deteriorates, due to 'noise'.

Put in the terms of the present hypothesis, it can be said that the Theory of Information, states that any message which has a meaning to its sender (for the present hypothesis, any load of ordered information) will lose its meaning while going through a communication system. This will be characterized by a similar process of decay described by the SLT. This suggests that 'entropism' becomes a general law. The 'load of information' in the framework of the present hypothesis is the distance or the level on the dimension of information, as well as the level of order, or information about information.

We have made a full circle and can come back now, to the general question raised already; why is it that all ordered systems, whether a crystal of snow, a set of cards lying on the table, or a chapter of the Bible which is transmitted over long distances, behave in a the same general way of disintegration, following the same form of law? The answer to this question as was mentioned already, is: a field of force. A similar reason to that which causes all bodies to fall, and all magnetic needles to point north. This means that the SLT is not more not less than a field equation, of entropy, in which the level of probability is proportional to the level of ordered information and vice versa. In daily life it means, that all systems of ordered information are under a constant tendency to disintegrate. The probability term in the general law, says that one has a smaller chance to come upon a highly ordered system than a simple system. It means also that you will always find out, that a single organized system is built of many simpler components, which each by itself has a higher probability to survive than the more complex system.

As was mentioned, Einstein described the field of gravity, in geometric terms, as space-time curvature, while the present model suggests to describe the field of entropy, as curvature of space-time-information (STI). Such a description as a matter of fact can be also named; the geometric description of an information system. The magnitude of any event, will be the size of the curvature or depression and the gradient of its surface. An observer, observing the event, will be another anisotropy or event or depression. If the two events have any impact each on the other, the type and magnitude of impact will be described as a funnel type curvature in the coordinate network system. In case the impact is on the behavior of the observer, the change will be in all three coordinates. The curvature in space-time relates to the material reaction, while the curve of the information coordinate relates to the mental impact. Yet one cannot separate them, because even if it is a mental event, it is combined with space-time processes, like electrical currents in the brain, etc. A series of events will be described as a sequence of depressions.

In order to help the reader to free himself from any anthropocentric impulses he still maintains, we may tell him that he himself, is not more not less, than a curvature in the network of space-time-information, (granted that the reader is accustomed to the idea, that from the point of view of weight, he is not more not less, than space-time curvature) part of the general curvature describing humanity, which is part of the more general geometric structure, describing the world of life.

As mentioned already, once it is claimed that all phenomena of spontaneous deterioration of order, in the universe, are a function of the existence of a general field of entropy, the SLT, becomes a partial description of the world, namely only of physical thermodynamic systems measured along space-time coordinates. This is done without taking into account the intelligent observer or physicist who deduces that law. One can say that the SLT, as explained and applied, in most text books of physics, is a partial picture of the real world. This partiality is due to the division between physical-chemical phenomena and that of perception, or between the observed physical world and its intelligent observer, following the already mentioned division between matter and spirit

This division, as discussed briefly, in the previous chapter, is an artificial one, and was introduced by Descartes in order to divide science and religion. It is thus proposed to try and eliminate this artificial division, which is a function of man's subjective attitude, and try to build an holistic world view. This will deal with the observer as well as with the observed as equal phenomena, from the scientific point of view.

It can be stated that the SLT which started, by the father and son Carnot, from the investigation of heat-engines, and was found later by Clausius and other physicist, to be of a general significance in the physical world, was examined only in regard to physical systems and not with regard to the physicist himself, who formulated, and looks constantly for proofs, for this law. If one argues, that a physical event which is not observed, is virtually not known, one has to include the observer and the observed in one isolated system. Thus the statement of minimum probability of spontaneous decrease in entropy of an isolated system, namely Boltzman's-Maxwell's formulation of the SLT, have to include Boltzman and Maxwell themselves. This brings the rephrasing of the SLT in the following way:

There are two states of extreme probability: the one of maximum entropy namely disorder and the other of minimum entropy (maximum nega-entropy) or maximum order. If one system is observed to move in one direction there is another system, which is observing it, and which moves in the opposite direction.

This rephrasing or restatement of the SLT, gives rise to an interesting situation, by which the three laws of thermodynamics seem to be interconnected. The First Law which states that the quantity of energy in the universe is constant, the Second Law discussed above (in its most shortened formulation; entropy is always in the increase) and the Third Law saying: At absolute zero entropy is zero.

The general formulation will be the following: Any change in the level of order of a system involves input or output of energy, which is equivalent to the rate of change of order The total rate of change is constant and is measurable between zero temperature, which is the state of minimum rate of change, to a state of maximum temperature (that of the Big Bang?) in which the rate of change is maximum.

To put these sentences in other words will be to ask ourselves whether we should not consider the universe as a general field measured along the dimensions of space-time-information (STI) in which systems of point-instant-notions (PINs), go through a constant change from order to disorder and vice versa, each change in one system is expressed or equivalent to the emission or absorption of energy, which is absorbed or emitted by the other systems.

This formulation is of course very general, but it has an important aspect, as it gives us the vantage point from which one can view and comprehend, within one set of dimensions namely STI, the evolution of the physical-biological, as well as the mental, or spiritual world. In the present chapter the evolution of the physical world was chiefly discussed, yet that of the biological and spiritual world was only touched upon, once and again, as there exists no sharp boundary between these worlds. The integration of the three worlds is claimed to be possible, if they are described within the framework of one system of dimensions of space-time-information.

I now propose to examine the creation of the world, or genesis from this new vantage point, which is within the field of entropy along these dimensions.

Before creation there was nothing, not even the dimensions were in existence, no space, no time, no information, and of course no information about information, namely no order. Then with the Big Bang, or any other event of creation, space-time-information dimensions were created. Space and time were formed, measurable along the dimension of mathematical logic and vice versa. This is to say that the dimension of information was created simultaneously, as mathematical logic, ingrained in space time. This was manifested also by the creation of point-instant-notions, or PINs, as quanta of observation.

In a more illustrative way one can say that at the instant of creation STI dimensions, which were squeezed into a singular entity, began to unfold. The unfolding or expansion was associated with a decrease in temperatures and in the entropy of the universe. PINs formed the new STI continuum. Yet one could not see any structure, namely differentiate between sets of PINs, as there was yet no matter. As temperature decreased the PINs got organized into the first particles like photons, electrons, positrons and neutrons. A stage further as temperature and thus entropy decreased, protons and neutrons got organized to form the most simple atom of Hydrogen and later by fusion the atom of Helium. At this stage the fields of forces called the strong-force and weak-force were manifested in addition to that of gravity and, of course, entropy.

All this development may have taken a minute after the Big Bang occurred. During the coming days while the universe continued to expand along the three dimensions, which meant; that more time passed, the spatial dimensions increased, and also the information increased. In the same time entropy decreased and energy was released. This meant (according to the new formulation of the SLT) a rise in the level of order which meant more composite structures either in space-time and information could be formed. As time is one directional, the increase along this dimension was the lapse of time. On the other hand space dimension enabled the construction of composite three directional structures. The bidirectionality of the information dimension, was manifested by the formation of composite mathematical relations between these structures, which meant also a higher level of order, or nega-entropy.

The further expansion of the universe along these three dimensions and the decrease in temperature and entropy allowed more complex structures, to form. After a billion years galaxies formed, going through a few stages from a cloud of particles to the collapse to a nebula to the formation of planets, one of which was our planet Earth.

Thus about 4.6 billion years the stellar body or planet named later by its inhabitants Earth (Erets in Biblical Hebrew) began to cool off, the rocks solidified, crystals of the different minerals were formed, releasing water as super heated vapor. As the temperature fell below the boiling point the first water bodies began to form together with a certain type of atmosphere, most probably quite different in its gaseous composition than the present one, but enabling, due to further decrease of entropy to form more complicated structures, which were the organic cells. These included a genetic code, which enabled them to generate their duplicates. From hence and up to date (and hopefully forwards on, along the three dimensions) life started, and continues, to evolve.

The evolution of the universe, as described above and which is based on the scenarios suggested by astronomers and cosmo-physicist (Hawking, 1988, Munitz, 1986) may change in the future. Yet in all future scenarios will remain the principle of evolution from a disordered primeval state to the more ordered state, which one observes today. This means a general trend of decrease of entropy, which is in contrast to the trend dictated by the SLT, described in a universal way. The reason for this being, that the evolution of the universe was activated by the energy of the Big Bang, which started as an explosion, from an initial state of disorder. This changed gradually as temperatures subsided. This dissipation was due to the expansion of the universe, as well as to the change from the state of plasma to that of matter. The same can be said about the individual celestial bodies, like our planet, after it cooled down and the minerals and rocks, we find on its surface were formed. The evolution of life on earth, is not a function of this general trend of cooling down. A new step, or jump, of organization has happened at this unexpected stage. Scientists are looking for an accidental incident of animation, to give the reason for this jump. Some think about electrical shocks, in the form of lightning, some speak about import of organic compounds from space, by meteorites, which does not answer the question how these compounds were formed somewhere else. Yet, as will be discussed later, the first impulse of formation of life, does not explain the continuing outbreak of the process of evolution of the world of fauna and flora. The model described in this book, however, forecasts higher levels of organization, once the level of simple molecules have been achieved. Granted a special impulse of energy may have been needed to overcome the general pull of the field of entropy, as well as to ascend a spectacular step of organization, yet the general arrow pointing to a higher level of order, once such a supply of energy was supplied is intrinsic in this model claiming a new field of force in which entropy is just a pole.

The reader may raise the question; how is it that the dimension of information, and entropy as a general field were not observed, by physicists? My answer, which was already touched upon, is that indeed they were observed, but they were expressed by other parameters, the main one being energy. According to the new definition, suggested above, energy is that, which one observes when there is a change in the level of order in the STI continuum. Thus, when physicists say energy, either production or consumption, I claim that they say, stepping up or down in the level of order. Thus all energy phenomena which are connected with the passage from one atomic structure to the other, are just an expression of the movement in the field of entropy measured along STI dimensions. This field along these dimensions, seems to me to express the most general field, in the framework of which, all other fields can be expressed.

This suggestion has also to do with the question of the arrow of time pointing in one-direction, which is observed as the flow of events from the future to the past. This puzzle occupied the mind of many philosophers and physicists (Reichenbach, 1971, Whithrow, 1961, Shallis, 1982). It is suggested that one considers the possibility that this universal arrow of time, which is interconnected with the universal arrow of entropy, is as a matter of fact, also connected with the movement forward, along the dimension of information, of any observer. This movement, spells always the increase of information about information. This increase in time, in order and space can also be described as the expansion of the universe along STI coordinates. This brings us as observers moving with the expanding universe to regard stationary features as moving backwards. Movement forward means simultaneously becoming older, being in another point in the expanding universe and being part of a system which contains more ordered observations. These ordered observations become more composite as the movement is towards the pole of maximum order. The illustration to back up this suggestion is that of an observer in a train which starts moving without a jolt. He is mistaken to think that the other trains in the station move in the other direction. When the train is in full speed and anything thrown from the window will fall in the space and of course in the time of the past. Keeping this illustration in mind and getting used to the idea that movement may be also along information, which is a dimension, and that information about information is order, the single direction characteristic to the arrow of time and entropy becomes more understandable.

In conclusion the conceptual model of the evolving universe which the reader is offered to consider, is that of a continuum of STI composed of an infinite number of quanta of point-instant-notions. This continuum was formed at the big bang and is in continuous expansion, influenced by different fields of forces which came to their expression when the conditions were suitable, which was at the instant the temperatures went below some 'threshold' value, At such a threshold the influence of the field of entropy, became apparent, affecting, most probably, the other four fields of forces. The field of entropy influenced any form of disorganization, organization and information. Thus this field may be considered as a candidate to the name of the super-field of force or even the general field of force.

The movement, or flow from a state of maximum entropy up the scale of negative entropy, or increasing order, is expressed in a certain stage, by the living organism and the story of its evolution.

4 Quantum physics, the dimension of information and the field of entropy

> He moves, and he moves not. He is far, and he is near. He is within all, and he is outside all.
>
> ISA Upanishad

The propositions of a new dimension and a new field suggested in the preceding chapters, may be considered by many readers as trespassing, by a geologist, into the fields of the physicist. This eventually raises the question whether such a trespass is legitimate, from a scientific point of view? This question was being asked, by me, throughout the process of the construction of the theory presented in this book. I was constantly aware of the fact that as this theory is built on geological-paleontological foundations, and myself being equipped only with the knowledge in physics required from a geologist, this invasion into other's fields may result in exposing ignorance, and performing embarrassing mistakes. As will be presently shown, the courage to continue with this venture, even after the safe grounds of geology were left behind, was picked up, from my observation, that problems in physics, which were known by me, to be in debate by the physicists, looked rather understandable, conceptually, when viewed through my new mental glasses.

As the reader by now is aware of, one of the main conclusions from the new space-time-information system of coordinates, is that information, i.e. knowledge and logic, believed to be in the realm of the spirit, cannot be separated from space-time, which is the realm of matter. On the other hand, while probing into the realm of physics, I was surprised to find out that this issue is under debate. This, even made me to suspect that the science of physics suffers from a self imposed mental constraint, namely a psychological barrier which does not enable bridging between matter and spirit. This conclusion became more established when I came upon the conceptual physical models, of quantum physics, which the physicists classified as 'weird'. When I applied to the issues under debate, the conceptual model, to which I arrived 'a priori,', I found out that my hypothesis suggested a conceptual logical solution, which later I found out, was already suggested by well known physicists, although they did not suggest explicitly that information is a dimension. During this stage of investigation I gathered more and more courage. This especially, as I came upon problems, which, I was not aware of their being an issue in physics, and finding out that the problems cropped up, independently, while I developed my hypothesis and most of them, were even solved, conceptually.

This brought me to the decision, to use these intersections between my theory and physics as test cases, for the predictability potential of my conceptual model. The reader is thus requested to bear with the author, and carry out a short survey of the various stages, through which the development of the model went through, and see for himself these test cases, or 'check-points'.

The first stage of the development of my model involved the suggestion to regard 'mind as a dimension intrinsic in space-time' (Issar, 1980). In the second stage, order was regarded as a dimension (Issar, 1982, 1984). At this stage observation was introduced as the smallest, finite quantum of any information about space time, namely as a Point-Instant-Notion or PIN. Order in general was then defined as constructions of quanta of PINs along space-time-information coordinates. This led to the conclusion that all the subject of information has something in common with the Second Law of Thermodynamics, as formulated by Boltzman and Maxwell. I was pleasantly surprised, then, to come upon the Theory of Information of Shannon and Weaver (1949), and to find out, that the basic equation for the potential of information-storage, or the rate of change from the original information contained in a message, to its outcome after passing through a noisy system, is equivalent to the SLT. The closing of the circle, in regard to the relation between the Information Theory and the SLT was my finding that there exists already a tendency among physicists to deal with thermodynamic systems, by applying the Theory of Information. (Tribus, 1961)

As already mentioned, another set of test cases or check-points, was with regard to the 'absurdity' or 'weirdness' of quantum physics. Examining the STI coordinates system, one can predict that any concept, which is in the domain of the intersection of the coordinates, namely where the 'point' forms a continuous entity with the 'instant' and the 'notion', as for example very small particles, very short events, or singular notions, one will not be able to define whether the object of observation is a spatial one, a temporal, or is just an idea. Moreover any measurement in this micro-domain which does not include the dimension of information may be 'correct' from the physical mathematical point of view but not 'understood', or absurd from the point of view of our daily experience. This in the first place applies to the involvement of the act of observation i.e. notion, with the space-time event, namely point-instant. Thus when I learnt about the 'weirdness' of quantum physics, which deals with events in the domain of quanta of energy, I was not surprised at all, and did not find it 'absurd', when I read that a particle, namely a spatio-temporal event, may be observed, at the same time, as a wave. On the whole, the phenomenon of quanta of energy, which had been introduced by the physicist Planck to answer for his measurements of heat radiation from a black body, looked logical, in the framework of the STI and PIN model. My model has already predicted, that there must be a finite smallest quantum of observation, namely the point-instant-notion or PIN.

Dealing with quantum physics brings us to the role of the 'conscious observer' in a physical event. As was already mentioned, my hypothesis suggests, that observation is intrinsic in space-time information, or STI. Moreover, all events which are observed (not necessarily measured) along STI dimensions, are under the influence of a field of entropy. This means that between the observer and the observed event exist similar relations to that, which exist in the field of gravity between two masses, or in an electromagnetic field between two magnets. This means that if a physicist performs an experiment, which involves processing of sense data, he progresses along the dimensions of time-information. It happens to him, by his mental effort of putting his observations into order.

The same model predicts, that when it comes to events in the domain of the quantum of observation, which is the point-instant-notion, or PIN, domain, that an observer is not merely influenced by the event he observes, but also influences it in some way. It is even claimed that the model predicts the 'uncertainty principle' of Werner Heisenberg (1971, 1974) which, as a matter of fact, ushered into the stage of physics the observer as part of the physical event. Thus the decision whether to observe the location, or the momentum of an electron, as well as to regard it as a particle or as a wave depends on the observer's decision how he would prefer to carry out his experiment or measurement. In the framework of the present model, one will say that whether an event will be regarded as a particle or a wave will depend on the dimensions to which the event is refereed. When these are space-information (time is regarded constant) the event will be grasped as a particle. When the event is measured along time-information (space is regarded constant) it will be referred to, as a wave. In other words the 'absurd' of a the interference of the decision of the observer with the observed is shown to become logical, once information is introduced as a dimension, and entropy as a field. The conscious observer, which is 'heavily laden' with ordered information, 'influences' the event, which is very 'light' with ordered information, like a heavy mass influences a very light mass. Moreover, if one is ready to admit information as a dimension to his physical model, he admits also probability as an intrinsic part of reality, as probability is proportional to the load of information of any system, as shown above, when the SLT in the formulation of Boltzman-Maxwell was discussed. In conclusion, the model claims that there exists no 'objective' science, but that the observer is a constant-intrinsic part of any observation. When an 'objective' observation is claimed to take place, it is just a partial observation, which might be correct but not an whole truth, like in the case of measuring a clock with a ruler.

The implications from the present model to the general problem of the relation between observer and observed, has also its implications in regard, to the great debate between the physicist Niels Bohr representing the 'Copenhagen School' and Albert Einstein. This debate can also be described as probability versus determinism in the exact sciences. The central themes in the theorization of the Copenhagen school of thought, presented by Bohr, Heisenberg and Born, was the 'uncertainty principle', mentioned already, which led to the formulation of the 'complementarity principle'. It states that two simultaneous, views or models of the same event, are legitimate from the scientific point of view. This principle was intended to give philosophical legitimacy, to the observations and hence the conclusions, regarding the duality of quantum objects, which relates to the fact that electrons, photons and other quantum objects behave like waves as well as particles. The way they behave, depends on the decision of the physicist how to conduct his experiment, which is; what and how, is he going to measure during the experiment. Einstein, who disagreed with the subjectivity, and unpredictability, which this way of thought introduced into physics, argued that what looks at present as fuzzy, or non-deterministic, is due to present methods of measurement and state of theory. He was convinced that once the instruments and theory are improved, the glory of the science of physics as a precise, deterministic theory will shine again. In order to show the self-contradicting results of the complementarity principle, Einstein, Podolsky and Rosen, suggested a thought experiment (the EPR experiment) in which one particle disintegrates into two complementary particles, flying apart. As each of these have equal and opposite momentum, and as their position is known, the measurement of either the momentum or position of one particle gives simultaneously the complementary information about the other. If the results depends on the decision of the physicist what to measure on one particle, then one has to assume either that the physical values are real and not fuzzy values, or that information is transmitted instantaneously from one particle to the other. If this is correct and the particles travel with the velocity of light in opposite directions, then one has to admit that the transmission of the information from one particle to the other is travelling in a super-light-velocity, which contradicts the special theory of relativity. Bohr's response was that the macro and micro systems cannot be divided, namely, all the space between the particles behaves like one entity, subjected to quantum logic. The two alternative paradigms were put to test by an experiment conducted by the physicists Aspect, Dalibard, and Roger in 1982. It consisted of polarization measurements made on pairs of opposing moving photons. The results of the experiment, show that indeed one photon 'knows' how its twin photon behaves. Thus if one does not admit super-light-velocity one has to admit that the results speak in favor of Bohr's inseparability paradigm, rather than of Einstein's insistence on separability between the particles, space and above all the physicist's decision how to perform his experiment. The applications of Aspect's experiment on the controversial questions mentioned above, were presented to leading physicists, by Davies and Brown (1986). Part of the answers are herewith cited, and the reader is asked to do for himself the comparison between these citations and the conclusions from the STI model discussed in the preceding chapters.

> If we're ever going to find an element of nature that explains space and time, we surely have to find something that is deeper than space and time — something that itself has no localization in space and time .... It is indeed something of a pure knowledge-theoretical character, an atom of information which has no localization in between the point of entry and the point of registration. This is the significance of the delayed-choice experiment. (John Wheeler in Davies and Brown, 1986, p. 66)

> No, it's a new kind of wave which I call 'active information'. The notion of active information is already familiar to us from

computers .... Now what I am proposing is that matter in general is not so different. (David Bohm in Davies and Brown, 1986, p. 128)

Another test case and I might even say prediction, applies to what is termed the 'anthropic principle' (Carter, 1974, Gale, 1981, Wheeler, 1976) This principle was asserted, in order to explain the strange coincidence between the creation and evolution of life on earth, and the basic cosmological conditions, which existed since the Big Bang. The 'weak anthropic principle' explains the fact that the same numerical relations are obtained from subatomic and cosmic phenomena. This value is in the order of magnitude of 10^{40}. For example the ratio between the age of the universe and the shortest time measurable is the same (i.e. the age of the universe expressed in units of nuclear time) as the ratio between the electrical and the gravitational forces for a proton and electron in a hydrogen atom, or the gravitational coupling fine structure constant, which is the ratio of the strength of gravitational to electromagnetic forces between protons. The age of the universe 10^{10} years, is the minimum duration of life of supernova, which is the basic constraint for the formation of the elements from which living organisms are composed. On the other hand if there was no life there were no physicists to calculate these constraints, or in retrospect the numerical value has a biological constraint. In conclusion the two ends of the universe the physical and biological are interlocked. The 'strong anthropic principle' insists that not only a particular numerical value is significant for the two-directional relation between the universe and its observer, but it seeks to explain that the presence of life is conditioned by the fundamental constants, and the later by that of life. Carter (1974) does not interpret the fact that there exist an interrelation, between the universal constants and life, as an evidence for the existence of a creator, which designed the world. He argues, however, that the peculiarity of the interrelations among the constants and its significance for the existence of intelligent life, is interdependent. In other words the existence of the universal constants, enables to predict the creation of life, and vice versa, namely, the existence of intelligent life enables to predict what will be the constants of the universe.

This theory came to my knowledge, when the present model was in a rather advanced stage, and thus the 'anthropic principle' which looked so bizarre to many scientists, seemed to me rather comprehensible. In the framework of the STI model it needed only rephrasing to become self evident. My suggestion is that instead of speaking of an observer better use the term dimension of information, and field of entropy. The physical meaning of the rephrasing means, that at the instant of creation, probably the Big Bang, the dimension of information was created together with space-time. This committed evolution to a process in which, intelligent observation became a necessity. As simultaneously the energy of the Big-Bang caused the expansion of the universe against the field of entropy to form more and more complex structures, composed of complexes of organized finite quanta of observation i.e. point-instant-notions. These, as discussed already in the preceding chapter, led to the formation of complex material structures, like atoms, molecules, and complex molecules. At a certain level, an organic, self producing molecule was observing its environment and adapting itself to the various conditions of the physical world. By this a new chapter opened in the history of earth, which is the chapter of the world of life.

5 Evolution, is it by chance or by necessity?

> We must therefore not be discouraged by the difficulty of interpreting life by the ordinary laws of physics .... We must be prepared to find a new type of physical law prevailing in it.
>
> Schrödinger, 1967, p. 86

At a certain time after the creation of earth, temperatures on our planet were low enough to allow water vapor to condense and turn into liquid and even freeze. Once a body of water was formed the hydrological cycle, started to move the molecules of H_2O in a circle. The water turned into vapor, which condensed into rainfall, part of the rainwater, either as streams or as groundwater, flowed back into the sea. On its route, the water dissolved particles from the rocks on which, and through which, it flowed, and became more saline. These salts accumulated in the oceans, together with other salts derived from volcanic emanations, and from rocks eroded along the shores, etc. During the eons which passed since the first molecule of water condensed, the oceans reached a certain salinity, which was retained up to present days. At a certain time some process caused the formation of a singular type of molecule in the ocean water. Let us concentrate now on this chain of events when certain inorganic molecules formed a more complicated organic molecule and this enabled the formation of a still more complicated molecule which was capable of self-multiplication. Phrased in thermodynamic terms, it can be described as the formation of a new system which could absorb energy and reduce its entropy or increase its order. Moreover, this system was able to transfer its competence of self organization and reproduction in the form of a coded molecule, namely the DNA, to its descendants. As time passed this system increased its order and complexity. From an organic complex molecule of DNA, it became a cell, which later formed a chain of cells to form one of the low-order living organisms. All the phenomena which were perpetuated from this humble, yet singular beginning, is what we call today the tree of life. The log book of this evolution is to be found in the assemblage of the fossils in the layers of rocks. The result of the fight for survival which started with the first living organism is the present biosphere.

The geological record does not, however, give all the sequence which is believed to have occurred. The main reason for this is the fact that only a very small part of the living forms were fossilized and preserved. For this the living creature needed to have either some hard component, or special conditions of preservation, which could have left its imprints on sediments which covered it. Unfortunately a long record of the most early forms of life was that of soft tissues, and on top of it the layers which were laid during the Precambrian era went through various degrees of metamorphism which have destroyed even the most delicate and fine imprint of any of these organisms which could have remained in soft clays. Thus all that remains are some ordered structures in the rocks of the Precambrian era of about a billion years ago. It is interesting to note that when such an ordered structure is found, arguments flare up as to whether it is a fossil of some archaic primitive organism or just some form of inorganic crystallization. The structures of these organisms, remind us of living colonies of bacteria and blue green algae. Later in the Precambrian one finds also algal mats (stromalolites). In the late Precambrian (600 million years ago) imprints of worm like fossils were found in Australia. (For a more detailed description of the first stages the evolution of the world life one is referred to Simpson (1983) and Bendall (1983).

At this stage I would like to restrict my comments on the problem of the creation of life, or how life began on earth, to its meanings within the framework of the STI dimensions and the field of order-entropy. It can be said that the creation of a more complex molecule than the inorganic one is predicted by this model, once the environmental conditions allow such an ascent. These conditions most probably arrived about 3.5 billion years ago. Whether it was in a shallow sea under an atmosphere rich in methane and ammonia, as believed by many chemists, or at a submarine hydrothermal vent, or any other environment, is a problem which is still under discussion by experts. What interests us is that the pull of the field to create a more complex molecule in space-time and, most important, information, existed all the time, waiting for the appropriate moment to be manifested. Here we come to the additional requirement which is the triggering factor. Whether an electrical pulse, or an impact by a meteorite or nuclear radiation, which is needed to jump the step between an organic molecule and a self replicating molecule. Assuming that the combination between the two requirements will be found sooner or later in one of the laboratories doing research on this subject, it is obvious that in nature it was a singular event, or a set of singular events. Otherwise we should have found signs of new beginnings of life, and their more evolved offsprings in our geological record. It might be still that nature is hiding a surprise, somewhere in some rock or in another experiment to produce life.

I do not propose to indulge in the question of what was the nature of the triggering impact which brought the beginning of life. As this is an issue which sooner or later will be solved and the process by which a molecule of RNA or DNA synthesized in a laboratory will take place. I would like to venture a hypothesis regarding this triggering impact. I suggest to the people involved in research in this field to consider the possibility that this impact was in the form of an ordered information shock, something like periodically ordered strong radio signals from a revolving celestial body like the quasars. [Or shock waves created by solar wind and earth's magnetic field. (*)] This may have caused a resonance of ordered information in a primordial soup rich in organic molecules, like amino-acids. A jump upwards in the complex organic molecules, such as proteins, along the dimension of information is what separates an ordinary organic molecule from a living molecule.

It goes without saying, that I am not suggesting here an experiment to test my theory. But I think, it will be a nice surprise if a daring chemist will be persuaded by this tip of information to involve ordered information in his experiment. This by preparing a soup of proteins and radiate it by strong, ordered periodic radio signals, and see if he receives some kind of a coiled structured self-replicating molecule.

Whether any laboratory test will succeed in producing life, the general question to be answered is whether the conventional laws of physics, chemistry, and biology will be sufficient to give the theoretical background for the continuation of the process of evolution from a primitive molecule to one of the higher mammals.

My claim is that at present there is a certain catch in the conventional approach of the physical and biological sciences which inhibits the formulation of such a new paradigm. I also claim that my hypothesis may serve as an opening, or as conceptual jumping-off point to such a paradigm.

In the first place I will try to defend my first claim, which I will call the catch of physics.

Let us fantasize now, that by some miracle, due to singular, excellent conditions of preservation, one of the very early cells have been preserved intact in a drop of water from the primordial ocean, in a rock cavity. Let us assume that this cell will be circulated between the best laboratories of biology, like the rock samples from the moon. The question which will be posed to the scientists in these laboratories will be to find the reason which caused or enabled this organism to form the multitude of evolved and complex structures known to exist at present. There is no doubt that most of the scientists will look for the reason or cause only in the cell itself. They will try to decipher its genetic code to find out what sub-code was responsible for the orders which brought about the multitude of forms known to the biologist. Some will try to find the formula of the counter impact or feedback from the environment on the cell and will argue that the many forms of life is the function of such a feedback process (Riedl, 1978).

Does not this attitude remind us of the attitude of people of science in pre-Newtonian times when asked to explain why an apple will fall from the tree to the earth? Did not they too, like contemporary scientists, looked for the force causing the apple to fall mainly in the falling object itself. At best, when asked whether they do not think a force from outside the apple caused the fall, they may have agreed that the wind was also responsible for the apple to be detached from the tree. None of these scientists would have looked for a force outside the apple, namely gravity, as something which pulls the apple towards earth.

Thus I claim that the focus of the attention of the scientists in the cell itself is analogical to that of the attention of science before the time of Newton in the apple, or in the weight or mass of the body to explain the observation of its fall. Newton, achieved his breakthrough in physical thought by transference of his attention to the space surrounding the apple. Although the mass of the apple itself remained an important component in the theory of gravity, the pull due to the mass of the earth generalized the phenomena observed in each apple. Einstein generalized this theory even further by describing gravity as a field of force analogical to the curvature of space-time.

Isaac Newton himself would have undoubtedly, argued against this suggestion, namely, that there exists an immaterial field of force, and no ether, between the earth and the apple. He needed this invisible ether, as a conveyor of the force of gravity between the earth and the apple, as well as between the heavenly bodies. Newton was not yet ready to think in the terms of a field of force, like that which Maxwell suggested for electromagnetism, and Einstein later adopted, for the force of gravity.

Two other forces have been admitted since then to the pulling-pushing team, namely the weak and the strong force, responsible for subatomic bonds. After these forces have been admitted, the door of the stable containing forces — namely gravity, electromagnetic, weak and strong — has been shut tightly, and no additional force has been added. All efforts have been implicated in merging the four forces into one general field of force.

Now when it comes to the formation of life upon earth and its evolution, the question is raised, why not look for a physical force which comes from outside as the one responsible for forming the RNA and DNA molecules in the first place. This force may well be responsible also for the evolution of the stupendous tree of life. Thus, it is hereby suggested to look for the reason for the formation and evolution of life in the space-time-information (STI) continuum surrounding this primordial cell, and not in the cell itself. The field of force which I claim to be responsible for this creation and evolution is the field of entropy, discussed in the preceding chapter.

The answer of most physicists will be (and as a matter of fact, this is the answer which I get when I discuss my hypothesis with an audience of physicists) that entropy, by definition, is restricted to thermodynamic systems, and it is not a field of force. My answer is that these definitions and restrictions are a snare, namely that the spontaneous movement towards higher levels of entropy by thermodynamic systems is not regarded as caused by a field of force, because it was not defined as such. The reason for this, in my opinion, is that the physicists need a psychological breakthrough, similar to that which Einstein considered as being essential, to grasp electromagnetism and gravity as fields.

As long as a physicist looking at a melting snow crystal, which is loosing its beautiful structure, does not ask himself whether it is not possible that the same principle — namely a field of force which causes the snow to fall from the cloud also causes the melting of the snow — if these questions are not asked, he will be moving in a vicious circle.

From my own experience I can advise him, that in order to arrive at this breakthrough, one has to start regarding information as a dimension, yet this was my path as a geologist, wishing to understand all that pertains to the intimacy between physics and the world of life, including, emergence of life, evolution, intelligence and thought. I claim, however, that even if one restricts himself within the boundaries of conventional physics, there is no reason not to regard the fall of a body from a higher level of higher order to a lower one, as a result of a pull of a field of force. There is the field equation, which, as already explained, is the Boltzman-Maxwell equation. Once one is ready to consider it, then there is no obstacle to make the second step, and say that as one needs the investment of energy in order to overcome the forces ingrained in the conventional fields, one needs to invest energy in order to overcome the field of entropy to produce life and keep it moving. This movement of life is recorded in its history, namely, its evolution from the simplest life forms, to the most evolved ones.

Suggesting that life is movement against the universal trend of increase in entropy, described by the SLT, was as a matter of fact, already done by the physicist Erwin Schrödinger (1967), who recommended we view life, or the living organism, as a system which feeds upon negative entropy, implying that organization is maintained by extracting 'order' from the environment. Yet although this is quoted in the introduction of many books in biology, I maintain that Schrödinger's recommendation quoted in the opening of this chapter, namely, that a new type of physical law should be looked for, was not given the attention it deserves. Especially so, when it comes to the processes of 'producing order from order' which according to him, characterizes living matter.

On top of this difficulty, there exists another one which physicists and biologists failed, to my opinion, to answer up to now. This is the teleological aspect, which is the programme imbedded in the process of evolution. This difficulty of explaining, through random mutations and selection by adaptation, the increase in perfection of instruments in living organisms, becomes even more difficult when the evolution of intelligence is considered. That the more evolved forms of life are the more intelligent, one needs no proof. That intelligence is an important tool for survival also needs no special effort of proof. The question is whether Darwin's theory, especially the principle of aimlessness (except the aim of mere survival) inherent in this theory, could have produced, intelligent behavior as a solution. Granted, that there exists a chance that an aimless, random walk may bring a drunkard to the door of his house, starting from a pub at the other edge of the town, this miracle will not repeat itself every weekend unless some slim plan of the town exists in the mind of the drunkard, which gives him some vague idea about his bearings and destiny. If this does not exist, then even if it works for one drunkard once, there are negligible chances that it will work twice, and there are no chances that it will exist as a general rule for the behavior of all drunkards in the world.

These difficulties of growing of complexity, interwoven with an apparent plan, were as a matter of fact intrinsic in the big change which Darwin's and Wallace's theory of evolution brought onto the stage of science. This was ushered in by Hutton and Lyell's theory of uniformatisms, namely by introducing the dimension of time into creation, and thus causing the tree of life to become dynamic, and in a perpetual *status nascendi*. This change did offer a scientific explanation for the existence of the variety of plants and creatures in nature, instead of that of a single, divine, perfect creation. The former philosophical, non religious explanation was that of Aristotle. It explained the tremendous variety of forms of life, by suggesting that there exists a teleological trend which is imprinted in nature. He philosophized that there exists some perfect creation of extreme harmony which is the mark or goal of all phenomena, partially expressed in the various creatures. Darwin's scientific theory of evolution through natural selection, which dealt and answered in the most satisfying way the problem of divergence and variety, left open the problem of the trend towards perfection which one observes in nature. An illustration to such a trend one finds in the human eye, not to speak of the brain; another example is the sonar system of bats. This problem is dealt in detail by George Dawkins (1986), in his book 'The Blind Watchmaker'. Adopting this as a phrase and the phrase 'The Cosmic Blue Print' suggested by Davies (1988), the question will be whether evolution of such intricate, efficient and striving towards perfectness instruments, as well as their concerted functioning, were created by a watchmaker who had no blueprint before his blind eyes. Another illustration will be that of scaling a ladder. Dynamic evolution showed that on the whole, the world of life started with primitive creatures, and that Homo sapiens, the most intelligent creature, was the last to appear on the highest scale of the ladder. Was, thus, the scaling of the ladder just a result of random mutations and selection by better adaptations?

Any analogical reconstruction of the scenario of the evolution of the living world, based on random appearance of forms selected by the big variety of environments, would undoubtedly have given the same number of varieties. The question is whether it would have given the increase in complexity, organization, and cybernetical management of the organism. This question was already illustrated in this chapter in the form of a mental experiment of finding a fossil primordial living molecule in a rock of Precambrian age, and examining it to ask whether the plan for evolution is imprinted in this molecule.

All these difficult questions brought about the proliferation of a multitude of theories. Jean Baptiste Lamarck was the first to suggest slow evolutionary development of the living world through acquired properties. The trend of the neck of the giraffe to lengthen while striving to reach higher trees is the best illustration to his theory. This explanation was rejected, as no proof was found that such a process exists. The Darwinian explanation was that changes through mutations are by chance, and that only those which give the creature a better tool of adaptation to the environment, survived. At present 'Lamarckism' has a negative connotation among biologists. Another explanation for perfectionism in the world of life was that of 'vitalism', introduced by the embryologist Hans Dreisch, who claimed that there exists a special force operating in the world of life. He called it 'entelechy'. This theory was supported by the philosopher, Henri Bergson, who suggested the *elan vital* (spirit of life) as the driving purposeful force, imprinted in all living organisms.

The contemporary paradigm, with which most biologists will agree is that of neo-Darwinism, which can be put in a nut-shell in the conclusion of Jacques Monod (1972): that since alterations in the DNA sequence, causing mutations, are accidental,

> they constitute the only possible source of modification in the genetic code, itself the sole repository of the organism's hereditary structures, it necessarily follows that chance alone is at the source of every innovation, of all creation in the biosphere. Pure chance, absolutely free but blind, at the very root of the stupendous edifice of evolution. (P. 112)

Richard Dawkins (1986) puts it in the following words:

> Natural selection is the blind watchmaker, blind because it does not see ahead, does not plan consequences, has no purpose in view. (P. 21)

The neo-Darwinist, no better than the Darwinist explanations, leaves open, in my opinion the basic question, already mentioned, which is at the basis of the mechanism of natural selection. This question can be phrased as follows: If one tells us that there is a process of production of alterations, or mutations, one has to admit also of some kind of a force to produce them. On top of it one has to explain the force which caused, in the first place, the RNA and DNA molecules to come into existence and to survive. In other words this type of force responsible for the existence and reproduction, which is unique for the bio-world, is taken as granted, and no explanation is offered to its intrinsic existence. No one will argue against the assertion that a DNA molecule is different from any other molecule, by its faculty to survive and produce mutations. What force is responsible, then, for these faculties?

Following Schrödinger's advice, quoted as the prologue to the present chapter, avoiding the help of a super-physical forces like the 'elan vital', 'enthalchy', or even a 'divine creator', we have to look for a non-conventional, physical law to be responsible for this difference between a non-living and a living molecule, rather than deny its very existence. Physicists introduced the nuclear strong force and the weak force when they had to explain the survival and processes of decay inside atoms. The electromagnetic force is involved in the bonds between atoms. So why not to consider a physical force coming into play when more complex self reproducing molecules, are observed.

As a geologist I have studied crystallography. In a book about crystals (Bunn, 1964) dealing with 'The vague borderland between the living and the nonliving, which the viruses represent' the author notes

> ... that the shapes and symmetries of crystals are characteristic of "dead" matter, they represent the most primitive kind of internal organization, a monotonous repetition of the same pattern unit in all directions of space. A living organism higher in the scale than a virus consists, not of many identical units, but of a variety of different units, each having its own form and function. (P. 281)

In order to gain the courage to push on with the idea of a new physical field which is responsible for the non-monotonous repetition of pattern which one finds in the living molecule, I am going to use an illustration from Dawkins' book 'The Blind Watchmaker', although its author apparently, needs no new field of force to explain evolution. He is happy with chance, only chance, and nothing but chance, to arrive from crystal to Homo sapiens. While explaining how this happens through the process of cumulative selection, Dawkins gives the following example:

> If you walk up and down a pebbly beach, you will notice that the pebbles are not arranged at random. The smaller pebbles typi-

> cally tend to be found in segregated zones running along the length of the beach, the larger ones in different zones or stripes. The pebbles have been sorted, arranged selected.

Dawkins goes on telling us that a primitive tribe living there will attribute the act of sorting to the a Great Spirit in the sky, while we, with a smile of superiority on our lips know,

> that the arranging was really done by the blind forces of physics, in this case the action of waves. The waves have no forces and no intentions, no tidy minds, no mind at all .... A small amount of order has come out of disorder, and no mind planned it.

What Dawkins has failed to note and to notice is that the arrangement of the pebbles is due to the combination between the force of impact by the waves, and the mass of the pebbles which is a function of the field of gravity. If this field of force would not have been there, the pebbles would not have been arranged in an ordered pattern. In other words, disorder by itself does not create order; one needs a field of force in order to produce order. In our case when only space-time is involved, the field responsible for the act of creating order is the field of gravity. My claim is that when it comes to an event which involves the dimension of information, one needs the field of force of entropy.

The field of gravity is involved also in creating order in living systems. This is in the case of the evolution of a fertilized egg to an embryo. It was found that the field of gravity is responsible for the determination of the bilateral symmetry of chick blastodiscs, (Kochav and Eyal-Giladi, 1971). This example where the field of gravity is responsible for putting order into an evolving life-form may most probably raise the question: why should one look for another field of force, in addition to the field of gravity, to be responsible for introducing order into matter (pebbles) and life, (fertilized eggs)? Indeed an attempt to show that the field of gravity is some kind of a general field, or even super field, responsible for the evolution of the cosmos to its present state, was already done (Gal Or, 1981).

My claim is that indeed the field of gravity is responsible for order, when events are measured along the dimensions of space-time. Yet, when it comes to the intelligence of the chick, this field will not suffice. One has to bring in a new dimension, i.e. information, and a new-old field, i.e. entropy.

Intuitively, I intend to claim that if there exists a general field of force, it is that of entropy rather than gravity. This can be seen also in the history of life, either of the individual, or of the whole tree of life. The conclusions from the experiments of Kochav and Eyal-Giladi (1971) with fertilized eggs, teach us to refrain from any act of fertilization inside inter-planetary vehicles, with no gravity field to give direction, as the outcome may be monstrous. It also tells us that the field of gravity had a function, when the first life forms came into being upon earth. Yet, when one advances to mature organisms, experience from two decades of space travel tells us that the absence of gravity has no crucial effect on the form of the travellers. On the other hand the process of organization along STI dimensions, namely all processes which involve movement against the pull of the field of entropy, are of crucial importance. These are the metabolic, as well as the intellectual processes. Thus, I claim that the need of the living travellers in a space vehicle to invest energy, either food, or heat, in order to stay alive, observe and think, tells us that the field of entropy is effective even when gravity is negligible.

With regard to the effect of this field on the evolution of the tree of life, my claim is, as already mentioned, that this is the factor which is responsible for progressive evolution. As a geologist, I claim that a 'random walk of mutations' does not comply with the paleontological evidence of simple organisms at the base of the stratigraphic column, and the evolution, stage by stage, into more complex and better organized systems as time progressed. A mere 'random walk of mutations' would have brought a directionless or 'neutral evolution' (Kimura, 1983), rather than the progressive evolution which brought to the emergence of the intelligent Homo sapiens. The neo-Darwinists who try to struggle with this non compliance by suggesting that more complexity gave better chances of survival, or in other words, that evolution from 'primitive' to 'progressive' living beings, gave advantage in competition, must also admit that there is a game of competition going on. Such an admission must also claim the goal or the name of the game, which is survival. This is in logical contrast with Monod's categorical assertion of 'blind chance.' Once there is a goal the competition gets a direction, and an intelligent observer can understand what the players are trying to achieve. Who has set this goal? How is the knowledge of the goal transmitted from one generations of players to the other? It is claimed, thus, that neo-Darwinists are not aware of the fact that 'competition' admits into their paradigm a 'vitalistic demon', which is a force which divides the living and the non living world. This demon pushes the first to compete for survival, while letting the second comply with the Second Law of Thermodynamics (SLT) and decay. There is no claim that living organisms violate the SLT, as they are open systems and export entropy, but one has to explain yet the mystery of the 'breath of life' which bothered intelligent man since ancient times (Genesis 2:7). Moreover, when the 'tree of life' is examined as a whole, one would expect, that its dominance in all physical system should have acted against progressive evolution. In other words, why did organisms continue to evolve beyond the level of simple DNA molecules, or at best, a microbe, or a blue algae? In the words of the physicists Professor Paul Davies, my arguments appear in the following form:

> I refer to the fact that the universe is progressing — through the steady growth of structure, organization and complexity — to ever more developed and elaborate states of matter and energy. This unidirectional advance we might call the optimistic arrow, as opposed to the pessimistic arrow of the second law. (Davies, 1988, p. 20)

These arguments are only an example of the difficulties, which many scientists, have in accepting neo-Darwinism, as a holistic theory. It is claimed that this theory, despite all of its magnificent achievements in explaining phenomena of invariance, heredity and complexity, is faced with a true difficulty of explaining 'progressive evolution'.

This controversy, or even paradox, between randomness observed in the micro-world, and directional evolution observed in global phenomena reminds one of the controversy, already discussed, between Einstein and the 'School of Copenhagen', headed by Bohr, regarding quantum mechanics. Einstein's statement, frequently quoted, in his letter to Born that 'He (the creator), does not play dice' (Pais, 1982, p. 443), summarizes it. In other words, the question whether the world is ruled by Chance or by Necessity is a problem shared by biology and by physics. I dealt with the latter in the preceding chapters, by suggesting that entropy regarded as a field of force along STI dimensions gives a conceptual-logical answer. When it comes to biology, my claim is that the same field and dimensions give the required holistic theory, which can explain progressive evolution in the macro-world, as well as teleonomy in the individual organism, while the micro-world is dominated by pure chance.

Paraphrasing it in the words of Einstein, I claim that 'He' plays dice with his left hand, while he puts order into the play with his right hand. Moreover I claim that the order put in by the right hand is according to a certain blueprint which is dictated by the disorder of the play of the 'left hand'. The code words for understanding the play are: The dimension of information and the field of entropy.

To explain this complicated paragraph I suggest a gadget I have invented for the purpose of teaching children the foundations of geometry. It consists of a box full of toothpicks, having a small hole at its side enabling only one toothpick to come out at a time. The toothpicks are of different colors, the number of colors according to the number of players. Each player chooses his color. At his turn, he shakes the box and lets a toothpick fall out. If its color matches the color he has chosen, he can keep it, tip its edge with a little glue and start constructing any geometric structure, a line, a triangle, a square, a cube, etc., the only constraints being that the toothpicks match in color, and are glued together only at their edges. Once the color does not match, the player has to return it to the box. The winner is the one who was able to build the most complex geometric structure. The shaking of the box and the mixing of the toothpicks is a continuous process of reduction of order, i.e. increase of entropy. I argue that this is analogical to the random play of subatomic particles and genetic mutations. On the other hand it gives a chance for the formation of new forms, by giving the chance for a toothpick of another color to come out, and once it matches the color the player has chosen, i.e. the environment, it builds a structure, which means that it reduces entropy by forming a more complex geometrical form. Starting with children in the kindergarten, there is a chance of having long snakes of tooth picks, when each end of each is glued to that of the other. As we advance with the level of the intelligence of the children, the structures become more complex and more sophisticated. Taking as granted that an analogical model does not conform entirely with reality, I hope it is enough of an illustration of the interaction between chance and necessity, in the continuous ascent from a soup of subatomic particles to the soup of organic molecules, to the formation of the primordial seed, composed just of a code of information, its evolution against all odds, from this tiny seed, into a flimsy bud, to become a gigantic structure of matter and spirit, perpetually ascending along the scales of ordered complexity, namely organization, the laws of which are intrinsic to the game. These are the laws of mathematical logic, of which Euclidian geometry, demonstrated in the game of toothpicks, is a special case.

The rate of growth of the tree of life is still in debate. Darwin's approach was that it is gradual, while today a group of paleontologists who believe in punctuational evolution (Stanley, 1981), will argue that the distances between the branches on the tree of life are some times very long, sometimes short. Yet, no one will argue against the fact that the higher one climbs on the tree, the more complex become its branches, leaves and flowers. I suggest we express this complexity by the reciprocal of Maxwell-Boltzman's formulation of the SLT, but instead of describing it as a thermodynamic system, it should be given Shannon's formulation for a coded piece of information, transmitted through a noisy communication system, which is the natural environment. Yet, my claim is that there exists a difference between an ordinary communication system (let's call it Bell's system, in honor of the company, which sponsored Shannon's research) and the one the code of life is being passed through (lets call it Darwin's system in honor of the man who braved conventionalism and attacks by the establishment). Along Bell's systems, the only relay stations allowed are those of electrical power, which support the power of the system but not the meaning of the message. The relay stations along Darwin's system support the system as well as the message, with negative entropy (or the children's intelligent mind in the toothpick game). In other words, the contrast between Bell's and Darwin's systems, is by the sign given to entropy describing the process the message is undergoing. One can say that in Bell's system where the sign is positive, the message is gaining momentum towards maximum entropy, namely chaos, while in Darwin's system the message is gaining momentum towards maximum ordered information. Undoubtedly the two systems act in the same field of force, which is entropy, yet the movement is in opposite directions. We can thus look at the genetic code of the organism as a built-in cybernetic directory which tells the organism to build a more complex organism in relation to the one which already exists. This can be compared to a Bell's system in which at each relay station, in addition to the power supply, there exists also a computer, which first of all repairs the message, adds some more messages and then makes it more complex. It will be easy to show that in order to build more complicated messages including more information, one needs more sophisticated computers. Is it possible to build a computer which will be able to build a better computer than itself? It is a debatable question between computer experts, yet even the scientists who claim that the building of such a computer is feasible will admit that in the first place, an expert having a plan for the basic algorithm is essential for this project.

Undoubtedly Creationists will assert that the mind of the child and that of the expert, referred to in the previous paragraphs, usher in a divine creator. They may be right if they are ready to agree that the creator can be described in terms of a field of entropy, having also a positive pole, effective along space-time-information dimensions. Thus, the introduction of the dimension of information and the field of entropy-order makes intelligence an intrinsic feature of the universe in general, and the world of life in particular.

But as the STI dimension system is a continuum, the evolution against the pull of entropy dictates also evolution along the morphological (spatial) features of the creatures, which means more complicated forms and less symmetry.

Thus, the question posed in the first chapter, which puzzled the author at the beginning of his career as a geologist, seems to be answered, namely that the change in the morphological features of the fossils must be interconnected with a change in their intelligence, as we are dealing with a continuum of dimensions and a general field of entropy-order. Once the movement up the scale of organization is disrupted, which occurs after the death of the organism, its form is subjected to the processes of decay, which is the decline in order and increase in entropy.

And from form and intelligence, one arrives at the question of behavior, which is the combination of these two features. The relation between these is that of a feed-back relation, which dictates that the progress in one direction is made possible by that in the other direction and vice versa. It can be said that the continuous need for survival against the field of entropy brings the organism to change its morpho-intelligent steps, the meaning of which is evolution of behavior; and when one of the components, either form, or intelligence, lags behind the other, the organism tries to fill up the gap by concentrating its effort in one front.

This feed-back mechanism is one of the most important features of life and is more pronounced, the more evolved is the form of life and its intelligence (Bitterman, 1965). One of the best examples is the evolution of the hands of the hominids parallel to the evolution of their brain and behavior. A similar relation one can find in other living systems, for example the property of smelling by dogs, the sight of nocturnal animals, or the sonic system of bats, etc.

Now for the understanding of the relation between instinct and intelligence. In addition to the definition of intelligence as a system responding along the dimension of information, the best description from the behavioral point of view is that of

> The ability to learn by observation, trial and error, or the ability to modify innate tendencies to react in certain ways to certain stimuli- tendencies based on neural connections between sensory and motor systems. (Bitterman, 1965, p. 92)

Instinct will thus be the neural connections imprinted either in the genetic code, when inherited, or in the brain, when acquired. The relation between these two properties in the context of behavior is similar to the relation between form and artifacts. While instinct and form are relatively conservative, intelligence and artifacts are flexible, undergoing changes according to the varying circumstances.

This brings us to the discussion of the problem of the 'selfish gene', a term introduced by Richard Dawkins (1978), who argues that the important thing in evolution is not the good of the species but the good of the gene. It is the gene that made the organisms act as its protector. All altruistic phenomena in nature, for example, the bee which stings the wasp, and pays with its life in order to protect the community, is just a performance of another device of its genes to protect themselves. The 'Selfish Gene' is logically interconnected with the 'Blind Watchmaker'. The basic paradigm underlying both paraphrases is that the tree of life is a result of a non-programmed struggle for survival. If there is any programme at all, it does not exceed the individual programme embedded in the genes. This explanation for the existence of the tree of life, contradicts, of course, the model proposed in the present book, which suggests that all phenomena of struggle for survival, and existence, including the shaping of form and behavior, is a function of one big programme, a function of the movement against the pull of the pole of maximum disorder in the field of entropy. This is manifested by the urge to create maximum ordered organisms, in form and behavior.

I have expressed already my reservations about the theory of the 'Blind Watchmaker'. These entail also arguments against the theory of 'The Selfish Gene' as both theories share the same principle, and express the neo-Darwinist paradigm of evolution due to the random walk of genetic mutations as shaped by the constraints of an antagonist environment. Concentrating my criticism on the 'Selfish Gene' theory, and carrying on with Dawkins' arguments *ad absurdum*; I would ask: why did nature (either blind or dumb, or both) decide that the gene is the unit which has to show such a determination to exist. It is apparent that if one examines the gene, he will find that it is built of organic molecules. Then why should one not say that the gene is a device of the organic molecules to protect itself. Continuing the examination down the ladder of structure of matter, one can repeat this question at each structural scale, down to the quarks. So all what we see in nature, carrying Dawkins' logic to its logical end, is a stupendous cathedral, built for the only purpose to protect the bricks it is made of. Once one reaches this conclusion, he asks himself whether it is not a matter of a personal subjective decision on how to describe a cathedral.

Another illustration for the logical absurdity of 'The Selfish Gene' theory will be that of a journalist interrogating soldiers during combat. Each soldier will tell him that his personal wish is to stay alive. The report of this journalist, will undoubtedly, ridicule all the strategical and tactical plans along which army historians will try to explain the battle. He will claim that he has been to the field, investigated the individual soldier, and knows the answer. Generals of the army would undoubtedly think that he did not have a big enough view. Biologists will claim that he did not have a small enough scale, as all the war was just a device of the selfish genes. I wonder what the atomic physicists will say?

In conclusion, once one admits that the gene, as self replicating and information containing molecule, is special in the sense that it is selfish, and transfers the selfishness to its descendants, one has to admit that there is a plan, which tells the gene to survive as an organism. How is this plan, or coded principle being implanted and transmitted from one gene to another? In the expected answer, one has to go to the logical end of his paradigm and explain, how this selfishness got there, in the first place, and how is it transferred in the second place.

Speaking in general terms, my argument is; that if one adheres to conventional physical laws, one will have to explain, first of all why is it legitimate, to suggest a field of force when it comes to the survival of atoms and molecules, and illegitimate when it comes to the survival of the living organism. Secondly, whether one admits that an additional field of force is essential or not, one has to explain the substance of the term information, being transferred from one gene to the other. If it is confined to space-time dimensions, then what should be the physical space-time instrument by which one can measure information?

Trusting that I have succeeded in pointing out, the difficulties which I have encountered, as a geologist, to accept the 'Selfish Gene' theory, I would like to answer a question based on the same rational principles which I have just stated, but directed towards my theory, that of a STI continuum, and a field of entropy. The question will be: how is it that this continuum and this field are not observed, when one goes to smaller structures than the living organism, namely to material molecules and atoms.

My answer, which was already touched upon, will be that indeed this dimension and field are observed, but they were expressed by other parameters, the main one being energy. According to the new definition, suggested already in Chapter 3, energy is that which one observes when there is a change in the level of order in the STI continuum. Thus any energy, income or outcome, observed while stepping up or down in the level of organization, as for example from protons to atoms, to molecules, to organisms, etc., are just an expression of the movement in the field of entropy measured along STI dimensions. This field along these dimensions seems to me to express the most general field in the framework of which all other fields can be expressed.

The numerous strategies for survival can be classified into two main groups (Eldredge, 1989). One comprises all those expressed in the reproductive strategy which try to survive by reproducing as much or more survivable off-springs. The other is the economic one, namely more adapted to convert better energy to forms and behavior enabling survival. I assume that many biologists will agree with me that with all the similarity between the principles of survival which one finds between the material world and the bio-world, an additional trend, namely that of evolution of intelligence characterizes the latter. This is expressed in the invention of new forms of behavior which modify the environment, for example hives, nests, and tools, as well as flocks, herds and tribes. All these structures and grouping involve construction, and thus involve a higher level of organization. Moreover the transmission of this capability to the descendants needs structured information. All these faculties are claimed to be against the trend dictated by the SLT. This law, when pronounced in terms of a field, is the trend to reduce the difference in the potential of energy between an event and its environment. Thus, while the general field of entropy is the one responsible for the production of various forms through mutational random jumps, the same law, but in the opposite direction, will serve to explain the construction of new forms when similar phenomena are regarded along the dimension of information.

This new framework embraces also the problem of chance in micro-evolution versus necessity in macro-evolution. What is defined as chance, or random mutations, is not more not less, than the influence of the negative pole of the field of entropy. This is manifested in the perpetual force trying to blur and smudge the differences in the potential of information, in space-time, between the various genes, or 'living bricks', resulting just in different forms (Dawkins' model). Against this general trend, works a force pulling towards the positive pole of the field of entropy, which is towards maximum ordered information in space-time. The result is all the different composite forms and levels of intelligence of species one finds in nature. Instinct or intelligence can now be explained as information for survival. This information is either embedded in the matter of the species, like the strong and weak fields in the atom, and is transferred with the DNA molecule. Or it is transferred by the teaching and imitation technique, the basic faculty for which is also embedded in the DNA. Its different variations, however, are transferred by a process of induction not much different than that of the induction of force by the field of gravity or electromagnetism.

This is a good opportunity to demonstrate the concept of the field of entropy-order in a space-time-information continuum. Let us consider a fully automatic camera. The photo-voltaic sensors of the instrument respond to the intensity of the light; by deciding the time of exposure as well as the diameter of the opening of the shutter. An acoustic sensor responds to the distance of the object by focusing the camera as well as changing the diameter of the shutter. An electronic chip regulates the orders from the two sensors. If we compare the performance of such a camera to that of an old box-camera, we can say that the modern instrument has more in-built instincts than the old one. Yet, when the conditions happen to be optimal for the setting of the box-camera, the performance as manifested by pictures taken by the two cameras may be rather the same. But once conditions change, the two instruments will react in a totally different way. The automatic camera will respond and adapt itself to the changes while the box camera will remain static. The principle of photography in the two cameras is the same, yet, their location on the dimension of information is different, the automatic one being situated on a higher level. It is also situated on a higher position in the field of entropy-order, namely information about information (This manifests itself also in the fact that there are more chances that a sophisticated camera will have a breakdown sooner than a simple box camera). Looking at the blueprint for the manufacturing the two cameras, it is obvious that one cannot find there all the future situations to which the cameras will respond differently, yet the way the instruments are constructed decides the way they will react. Correlating the instruments to living creatures, one can compare the blueprints of the cameras to the DNA code, where the level of complexity of the future reaction is written, while the operators which decide the exact way of reaction are distributed all over the instrument or body. Thus, for example, when we go down the levels of the ocean, the light receptors of acquatic dwelling creatures change in molecular structure in order to intercept lower and lower intensities of light.

The endocrine systems of birds that are migratory begin to operate according to the length in hours of daylight (*). When speaking on instinct and intellect, one can correlate the reaction of the automatic camera to that of the instincts of a living creature. The resemblance will be also in the way it will react to a new situation for which it was not designed, for example, radiation of a different wave length than seen light, like for example x rays. In this case only if there is an intellect backing up the instrument or creature, there are chances to change the behavior according to the new situation.

In conclusion, what is called the behavior of the Selfish-Gene is not more not less than the manifestation of a local, temporal balance between the various fields of forces, the general one being that of entropy. This is manifested by the tendency one observes in all levels of structures, whether protons, atoms, molecules, or small blocks, to maintain their existence. When some of these particles, blocks or species have a strong force of cohesion between their components, they will regarded as conservative. If fortunate, due to its being located in a niche protected from the destructive force of the field of entropy, they will succeed in this state; if not they will disintegrate. Others will 'try' to survive by changing their form-shape or behavior.

Thus the complicated ways, systems and patterns of evolution become simple. They are the bobbing, jumps, movement flow and reshaping of the blocks-creatures in a pool, adjusting themselves to the pulls in different directions of the various fields, dominated by the general field of entropy, having two opposite directions, or poles, namely maximum and minimum order.

Saying that the field of entropy is the general field is not saying that it is the strongest one. It says that it is present every place all the time in a potential to act in the two opposing directions. Yet local conditions enable the other fields of force to overcome entropy. For example, If blocks in a pool have small magnets, one will see that, in contrast to the pull of the field of entropy to structures to fall apart, once two blocks come close enough within the influence of one magnet on the other, they will pull or push each other. Once they were adjusted in a way that the north pole is opposite the south pole, they will tend to attract more blocks to form a bigger block resisting the other forces to tear it apart.

Life is manifested when there exist also the environmental conditions which enable the pull of the positive pole of the field of order-entropy to overcome the pull towards entropy. This happens when this force is the strongest one, and also when an optimal local environment, like that which is found on the planet earth, exists. Thus when one observes living creatures in a pool, he observes the reaction to this force. The more composite the structure, the more complex will be the reaction. Thus, green algae, while reproducing, will form algae mats. More evolved species may form colonies. In the mating season the males and females will seek each other to reproduce. Thus, the whole process of reproduction can be described as the integration of separated information structures, forming separate bodies, into more complex wholesome structures. The best illustration is, of course, the fertilization process of the egg in the womb. One does not need a mysterious force of vitalism to explain this tendency to act against the field of entropy. It can be explained by the same field but in the opposite direction, namely the direction of more order, which is being manifested, when investment of energy is secured.

The understanding of all the phenomena in nature, of disintegration into more simple structures and construction of more composite and intelligent systems, (including that of life) as the interplay between the various fields of forces, still leaves us with the question: what are the special conditions which makes the big pull of evolution of life overcome the pull of the negative forces. The clue to the answer can be found above in Chapters 3 and 4. I maintain that these conditions are imbedded in the evolution of the universe since the Big Bang or moment of creation, and specified by the anthropic principle. This principle, interpreted as the creation of the field of entropy along STI dimensions, is a continuous flow towards the positive pole of entropy, expressed continuously in more and more complex structures of quanta of observation, namely PINs.

To help the reader visualize this, it is suggested that he imagine that in addition to the fact that all the molecules building blocks of wood floating in a lake are magnetic, there exits also a big and very strong magnet at the edge of the pool. Sooner or later the blocks and their parts will find a way to come and concentrate at this edge, fighting their way against the forces of all other fields. The negative pole of this big magnet, in nature, is the negative pole of entropy, which is the black hole of chaos. This is the state in which order along space-time-information approaches zero. This was probably the state of the universe at the moment before the Big Bang. The positive pole of the magnet of entropy is just the opposite, namely, maximum ordered information in space and time. The force triggering the movement towards this pole was the Big Bang. This movement on earch is maintained by the constant inflow of solar energy. The processes of the absorption of this energy, the construction of the organisms and the resistance against the pull of the negative pole, is what is called by the biologists the struggle for survival and multiplication.

6 Survival and ethics

> There is only one path to peace and security: the path of supernational organization.
>
> Albert Einstein, in an address, on the occasion of receiving The One World Award, April 27, 1948

As was suggested in the last chapter, the living organism should be regarded as a complex structure which reached a high level of negative entropy (positive order) in the field of entropy. It can also be described as a system with a high degree of information, constructed along space-time information (STI) dimensions. Its creation in the first place was due to the expansion of the universe due to the initial input of energy of the Big Bang. Its survival against disorganization, dictated by the second law of thermodynamics (SLT), is due to the constant input of solar energy. (Organisms in the depth of the oceans get their support from sub-marine thermal springs). Thus the first outburst of energy at the moment of the creation of the universe enabled its take-off from a state of maximum entropy or total chaos. As evolution progressed, organization manifested itself in an escalating order, from observation quanta or point-instant-notions (PINs), to elementary nuclear particles, atoms, molecules, organic molecule, to the gene, cell, multi-cell organisms, like corals, etc. As one goes up the tree of evolution, organization of individual organisms into societies becomes more apparent; and, indeed, one can regard the organization of the social insects, like the ants and the bees, as one organism divided by space.

Anytime a few organisms cooperate, there must be some specific behavioral rules which enable them to unite and at the same time to reject other creatures from interfering with their cooperation. In some instances the cooperative grouping involves also territorial claims. The levels of organization are different from one type to the other. Many creatures will prolong it to the period of nesting and feeding the young while others will retain it all their lives. The size of the organizations as well as the behavioral codes are characteristic features of the species as its form. As was mentioned, the honey bee and the ants have developed a very complex social system. Yet its behavioral code is instinctive. As one ascends the tree of evolution he will reach societies which interact in an intelligent way, which means that they transfer the codes of behavior not by genetic transfer, but by training their young to behavioral patterns.

In very evolved animals like the primates the codes of behavior become rather complex and training through initiation is in many instances human like.

When the Homo-sapiens level is reached, an ascending degree of organization can be observed also. The most simple group is the family a more complex society is the tribe. A few tribes may cooperate to form a nation. In most cases the act of organization involves also territorial claims and thus, villages, cities, states, and kingdoms were formed.

As was done in relation to the evolution of the form and behavior of the different species in the bio-world, it is suggested to regard the evolution of grouping and organizations in this world in the framework of the field of entropy-order, along STI dimensions. This explains, to my opinion, the hierarchy or complexity as well as the behavioral patterns which characterize societies of animals and men.

It can be said that the same force which pushes particles to come together to form a body, pushes bodies to come together to form a society and the complexity of the binding forces or laws between the components will be a function of the level of order, or information about information which the components of the society reached. The higher the level, the more complex are these laws.

Yet with all the complexity, a few characteristic and common basic rules can be identified in all levels of organization, similar to the basic rule which decides the structure of the DNA which can be found in all forms of life. The basic rule in the case of societies is that some level of harmony has to exist between the individual members. In other words there is a give and take agreement, or balance of interests between the individual selves. Once this 'feed-back' system deteriorates, the structure crumbles. This harmony, or balance is, as a matter of fact, the manifestation of the equilibrium between the two opposing arrows, one towards entropy, the other towards negative-entropy, or order, discussed in the previous chapters. The action of the arrow towards more order is expressed by the increase in the complexity of the structure of the society, and at the same time, intricacy of its laws.

Biologists explain the same phenomena by conventional sociobiological terms without involving entropy. Their basic principle says that the groupings into social structures gives a better chance of survival and thus will be adopted as one of the strategies of the preservation of the species (Wilson, 1975). The 'harmony' between the individual animals in a group dictates a certain amount of concession of selfish interest. In its extreme, these concessions will amount to self sacrifice of one individual in order to save the society. As cases of altruism do not concur with neo-Darwinism, as asserted by the theory of the Selfish-Gene, it is understandable that the advocates of this theory will try to show that altruism is not more, not less than disguised selfishness. Here we come to a vicious circle of the type of questions: what was first, the hen or the egg. As the code word is survival, sacrifice of selfish interests, namely altruism, will guarantee the survival of the group, which guarantees the existence of the gene, which guarantees the survival of the individual and the circle turns round again. As already suggested in the preceding chapter, I am asking the question; why stop at the level of the gene and not proceed to the level of the organic molecule, etc. until we reach the level of the quarks? Fortunately, for the time being no smaller particle is known (unless the reader is ready to adopt the PIN, as the smallest quantum of observation) and thus the vicious circle is cut, by deciding that all phenomena of existence are devices of the 'selfish quark'. In order to avoid this *ad-absurdum* reasoning, it was, and is suggested also in the case of altruism, to adopt the holistic approach to the various strategies of survival. This means that phenomena of selfishness on one side reveal the pull towards deterioration, namely towards a minimum level of order, while altruism discloses the trend towards maximum order, which are in this case organized societies.

The same goes when one comes to the explanation of the processes which cause the formation of societies. The neo-Darwinists, who believe in chance, or random processes, as the basic agent in evolution, will argue that only by pure chance some organisms found cooperation to give them an advantage in the competition for survival. Here one enters again the vicious circle, rotating from egoism to altruism, and vice versa. The argument that once a few individual egos cooperate to form a society, each of them has to compromise his egoistic interests in order that the society will survive, amounts, (as we learn from many societies in the living world) to self sacrifice, which causes the elimination of the individual ego, which is against the reason that the society was created in the first place. As already discussed, disciples of the Selfish-Gene paradigm will explain self-sacrifice by claiming that this act saves the genes. This brings us back to the question already discussed, namely, why is the gene the chosen as the consecrated system, and not the organic molecule below him, or the living organism above him?

In order to avoid this vicious circle, which starts with the everlasting conflict between chance and necessity, a more general model will be suggested, this time for social organizations, to reconcile between these two contrasting arrows in an holistic way. This will involve abrupt transitions from the inorganic and animal world to the world of human history and vice versa. These transitions may be found difficult to be accepted by many people who regard history, sociology and even socio-biology as non objective sciences; as evidenced by the lack of agreement between historians and other social scientists as compared to the consensus arrived at by physicists. My answer is that this difference which seems to exist between the physical-chemical and social sciences (and I include history in the social sciences) is due to the difference in complexity and scale. Let me explain this. I claim that physical-chemical phenomena are relatively simple when compared to social phenomena. One has to remember that every individual member of any living society, is composed of billions of organic molecules, each of which is a complex of many inorganic molecules, etc. The more composite is the structure, the more complicated is its behavior, which is expressed in the abundance of states of freedom. The only way to relate to these is by the statistical approach which depends on the availability, quantity as well as by the methods by which data is collected and interpreted. On top of it comes the fact that the observer is part of the system, either physically or mentally or both. In order to convince the reader that this is the case, I suggest that he compares two types of measurements, one will involve the change in the volume of a mixture of gases due to heating, the other the change in a the habits of a certain community to a higher standard of living. Although there will be no arguments between the physicists regarding the results of the physical measurement, we know that its precision is a function of the number of readings of lengths and temperatures made. The more the readings the more will the physicists be satisfied with the results, which will be the average of the readings. This when the precision of the instruments, and the conditions in the laboratory are according to the standards agreed upon by the physicists. The picture will look different when the physicists will be in the size of a gas molecule and will have to do the same experiment while jumping with the other molecules questioning them about their velocity and the lengths of their trajectories. On the other hand regarding the measurement of the habits of life, once the sociologists agree that the standard of measurement will be the number of private swimming pools, as measured on an air photograph, taken before the rise in the standard of living, and later on, the agreement about the results will be more or less the same as in the case of the gas.

If one agrees that even though there exist differences between the physical and the biological worlds, yet the trend of increase in organization is observable in the two worlds, then once a certain observation repeats itself one should start looking for the general law. Thus, if different societies of animals show the same tendency of forming colonies, hives, nests, herds, families, harms, tribes, nations, kingdoms, etc., then it is not a random event any more, but a manifestation of a subtle, hidden general trend.

Yet, remembering that a trend of deterioration exists also, as expressed by the Selfish-Gene principle, the apparent contrast between these two opposing trends should be explained too. Both phenomena, that of the trend of association, as well as that of individualization, should be tried to be expressed by one general law. In other words when one scientist says that his observations point to one direction and the other scientist claims that the data he accumulated, points to an opposing direction, a third direction which complements between the two opposing directions, should be searched for.

The reader may guess, correctly, that the holistic-complementary model which I would suggest is that of the field of force of entropy which contains also the arrow towards maximum order or negative-entropy. Obviously, since I am prejudiced in favor of this model, I will argue that the agreement or reluctance of the reader to accept this model, depends on his subjective attitude, namely on his agreement to surrender the last trench of anthropo-centralism. I imagine that the reader may well be aware of the inevitable conclusion towards which this model points, which is that all moral values at the basis of our society are not more than the manifestation of the forces in this field. This conclusion is especially difficult to be accepted by those readers who connect moral and social laws with divine and supernatural forces, thus making the social code of behavior a religious issue.

This difficulty is understandable, once one takes into consideration that the anthropo-centrical attitude, by itself, was a tool for survival. This manifestation of selfishness was on all the levels, from the individual, to the tribal, national and even that of the species, which in our case, is the Homo sapiens. Thus, by seeing themselves as the center of creation, man, tribe, nation, humanity, were encouraged to further their selfish interest, on the account of any other living society. The gradual extrication from the anthropo-centric pull comes in the evolution of the individual, as well as society, with the progress along the dimension of STI, namely the increase, as a function of time, in ordered information, which is intelligence of the individual and society. It comes with the gradual replacement of instinct by intelligence. This can also be described as a general progress towards a better understanding of the world.

The reader who is willing to free himself totally from his anthropocentric bonds, should consult the books which deal with the evolution of man's culture since early prehistoric times, for example, Leakey (1960), Clark (1977), and Clark Howell (1970). These books will help the reader to descend the ladder of the evolution of man and human society to the most early levels of prehistory. Although it is still debatable what were the exact stages along which prehistoric societies progressed on their route from primates to agriculturists (Isaac, 1983), nobody will argue that during the Paleolithic period, which started about two million years ago and continued over most of the stone age, the level of organization was not more than that of clans and tribes hunting and gathering food together. Only since the Epi-Paleolithic, starting about seventeen thousand years ago, and certainly at the Neolithic period, starting about ten thousand years ago, one finds material evidence of settlements which comprised a multi-family or even tribal organization.

The correlation between the material evidence from extinct prehistoric cultures, like the remains of flint tools, distribution of shelters etc., and results of sociological studies of 'fossil' cultures, which are still hunter-gatherer societies, and which survived in ecological niches, like the aborigine tribes in the tropical jungles, show that indeed these societies get along quite well with an organization not bigger, nor more sophisticated than a clan or a village, forming a loose bond between a few families. The passage into an agricultural society demanded a more elaborate and permanent social structure for enabling the distribution of limited resources like land and water. This initiated the formation of hierarchic structures, first in city-states and later in kingdom-states and empires.

If one examines the brain sizes of fossils, the hominid record shows variation and increase in complexity, rather than growing within the species. This is the case when one finds one subspecies living in the same time as the other, for example the Australopithecus boisei and the Homo habilis (Eldredge, 1989). At the end of the Last Ice Age, (namely the end of the Pleistocene, beginning of the Holocene, 15,000 to 9,000 years ago) the shift from hunter-gatherer, to pastoral-nomadic and agricultural-villagers societies, took place. This occurred when the only human species (found up to now) was the Homo sapiens. This means that speciation into behavioral groups was not according to brain size but some other reason. One still finds, as a matter of fact, differences between the races in their form, like color, shape, etc. (Dobzhansky, 1962), but in general one can say that speciation went more according to different socio-economic, and socio-cultural groups, namely behavioral patterns. These changes were more a matter of software, rather than hardware. Thus, the Darwinist principles of evolution were not abolished at the appearance of the Homo sapiens, they were and are shifted to changes in the software, which is manifested by socio-economic-cultural structures. For example, the cases where different societies of different social and cultural levels, fighting for domination over the resources in their mutual habitats, should be explained in the same terminology as one explains the fight between different species or sub-species differing in form. Yet we know from archaeological evidence that this fight was not only by force but also by skill, which was also pronounced by developing better weapons, and more advanced social organizations. There was also a transfer of skills from one society to the other. This took place when some kind of equilibrium was achieved and one society started to imitate the more successful one. These skills and organizations were transplanted from one region to the other. This happened when a particular society had to migrate to a new environment due to some kind of pressure, whether from another human society, or due to the overcrowding of the inherited habitat, or due to changes in the natural environment. When a certain society changed its way of life in a new environment, it still continued with some of the traditional social laws and social agreements its ancestors developed. For example, a hunter-gatherer society which managed to harness fire, and which depended on it and thus deified it, (or as result of its feelings of awe, or just to ensure that the women keep it ablaze) will continue to worship the fire, giving it another meaning, even after adopting an agricultural way of life. They might have added later the water and the soil as divine entities but still maintained for a long period the fire as one of their gods. The same can be said about social laws and taboos which were formed in order to maintain the ancestral societies from disintegrating. This reminds one of the principle of conservatism, characterizing the evolution of the gene and species.

Thus, it is claimed that the evolution of different forms of societies, with different socio-economic-cultural characteristics, does not differ from the general scheme of evolution of the spatial form of the species. This includes not only behavioral but also moral codes. In other words it is argued that the laws which decide the survival of social-moral codes are not different from those which decide survival of inherited codes deciding the forms of animals, as well as their behavior. The only difference between a code of survival by the change of form or instinctive behavior is in the load of ordered information in the genetic code. Thus, all the different strategies to guarantee survival of societies, both animal and human, are just another way to work against the arrow of entropy. This arrow, in the case of human societies, is to cause them to disintegrate, morally and thus socially. Such a disintegration is the basic danger to survival.

In practice, one of the strategies of survival was to identify all that is working to keep society intact, namely all that works against the arrow of entropy, to regard it as good and divine. Thus heroes fighting to protect the society were deified, and elders suggesting laws for binding the society together were called prophets, judges and holy men. In time of peace they were made leaders. On the other hand, all that was working for entropy was labeled as bad, and as coming from some negative force in the world. This evil force caused many problems to the human mind. Already in ancient times people observed that this negative force is equal if not stronger than the positive one. As a matter of fact, each man had, in this or that way, his personal experience of two impulses, one to cooperate with his society even when it means sacrifice of his own interest, and the other to take advantage of other people in order to advance his selfish needs. In other words, the idea of the Selfish-Gene became manifested in the idea of the selfish or evil individual.

Various societies have developed different solutions to explain these contrasting pulls one towards good, the other towards evil. In the pagan periods good and evil started from the gods who were divided into the good ones and the bad ones; while the goodies helped in the positive direction in protecting and promoting the existence of society, the bad ones did their best to advance destruction and chaos. One finds in most ancient mythologies the primordial fight between the good god protector of the society and the bad one, wishing to destroy it. The fact that the society exists was evidence to the victory of the positive force and this had to be celebrated. The holy days were an opportunity to narrate the story of the war between the good and bad and pay tribute and swear allegiance to the protector. The anthropo-centric pull, namely the 'selfish self' direction, made man create personal and family gods to be worshipped daily. This had a positive influence; it spelled personal responsibility. In many societies this may have been a continuation of prehistoric times when the spirits of the ancestors, personified by their skulls being present in the dwelling area, were keeping watch, and were responsible for the continuous existence of the family.

This conflict, of complimentary quality between good and evil, general and individual, finite and infinite, one finds in most of the ancient cultures of the world; its conformity with the main issues of modern physics is demonstrated in the most dashing way by Fritjof Capra (1975) in his book The Tao of Physics.

The wars between societies, namely the fight to achieve more resources and expand in space, was declared as a war among the gods. And the god who was more successful, had more followers. Conquests, and other close contacts between societies led to the transfer of information from one society to the other. This led to the adoption of beliefs, gods, rituals, many times while changing names. This enabled assimilation and integration of societies into bigger ones.

As one speaks about one species, interbreeding promoted assimilation and thus new societies were formed which were the product of genetic and cultural assimilation. The two strategies of fight for survival are also apparent in this direction, while some societies exercised the 'selfish self' direction and imposed taboos on cultural and sexual interconnections with other societies, others were assimilators trying to spread their genes and culture as much as possible.

It is interesting to note that the efforts to explain good and bad were always connected with the effort to explain the genesis of the world and man. This may be due to the fact that the knowledge or understanding of the world is just another facet of the arrow against entropy Thus the effort to expand along the dimension of information up the gradient of the field of order was by building socio-cosmological mythologies.

The desire for a more ordered world view led to the development of Monotheism. It started from one god seizing sovereignty over the other gods and dictating his will. In a more advanced stage, when man started to grasp the world in a more abstract way, the supreme power became also a symbol of justice. It was He who has given the laws which have to protect the society from its enemies inside and outside, namely from the arrow of entropy pointing towards disintegration. Yet even the laws of the abstract god contained many of the ancient taboos and rituals inherited from the more primitive stage of the society.

One will find an example of such a development in the comparison between the more ancient story of the deluge as told in the Accadian-Sumerian epic of Gilgamesh, to the very similar, but succeeding story, found in the Bible. In the Gilgamesh epic, the deluge is explained as just a whim of the gods, while the biblical story gives injustice of society as the reason for the catastrophe. The two stories are a result of a humid climate change, which occurred about five thousand years ago, and which brought rain and floods on the arid lands of Mesopotamia (Issar, 1990). The sacrifice of animals by Noah, after deliverance, is an apparent stigma, from prehistoric times.

We may look thus, upon the religious and cultural history of society as a struggle between the evolutionary trends, of the 'selfish self' and the 'social gene', the first as revealed in the tendency to retain the national beliefs, rituals, etc. and the latter, in the desire to learn and adopt ways of thought, beliefs and even rituals from other societies. These two opposing tendencies are modifiers of the general course of evolution, towards a more complex structure of the society, and a more sophisticated world view.

Thus when one surveys the evolution of nations, one will find the same contrasting tendencies, which are characteristic of the evolution of organisms and species: on the one hand the trend of disintegration and the splitting of societies due to cultural diversification, and on the other hand the desire for the agglomeration into bigger and stronger unions and states. Yet the more advanced the society on the dimension of information, and the higher up it is in the field of order, the more this unity is expressed in a mutual advanced, cultural background. The more primitive the society, the more evident will be the symptoms of unity. The disintegration of societies, is either due to the SLT, which causes diversification in culture and religion, as well as of the trend towards unity. The evolution of nations, their religions and laws, is thus the same as the evolution of species, but while the forms of the believers remains the same, their belief and behavior change. It is interesting to note that in many cases the change in religion is parallel with a change in garments and other symbols to emphasize the difference between people who otherwise look the same.

The similarity between the diversification of species and cultures can also be seen in the degeneration and decline of cultures, once they were not able to adopt changes and leave behind primitive beliefs and rituals.

This chapter is not intended to give the history of religion and cultures of mankind. Its aim is to demonstrate that by adopting the space-time-information dimensions along which the field of entropy-order is measured, one can grasp the evolution of religion and culture in the same framework as that of evolution of species, namely towards more ordered, organized and at the same time diversified groups.

The different behavioral patterns characteristic of each culture and religion which are the function of the pull of the two contrasting arrows of the field of entropy-order, one to diversify into smaller and smaller groups and the other to get organized into bigger societies, is expressed in all the levels of organization, having positive and negative effects. Thus the deterioration of a society into too small groups is dangerous, as each small group cannot withstand pressure from outside, while the building of too big groups may also be dangerous as the coherence weakens, and it cannot withstand the pressure from inside and outside. To these inborn forces, one should add pressure from the natural environment, like climate changes, which may cause frosts, floods, droughts, which may bring in their wake, famine and the invasion from the stricken lands to the areas where food and shelter can be found. Outbursts of epidemics may be another reason for disintegration of societies.

The evolution of humanity can thus be regarded as a continuous struggle to find an optimal route between all these pulls and pushes. The survival of ancient cultures, religions and beliefs on one hand, and the explosive evolution of science and modern ways of life on the other hand, are thus not more not less, than manifestations of conservationist strategies on one hand and punctuated jumps of the evolution of the Homo sapiens species, on the other hand.

If this is true, then it can be anticipated that in the near future, historians, sociologists, biologists and paleontologists, will submit interdisciplinary research proposals to investigate the processes of 'spiritual' evolution in the bio world. The word 'spiritual' is put in quotes, as it expresses my belief that the wall dividing 'material' and 'corporeal', and 'spiritual' and 'divine', does not exist. It is just an expression of our anthropo-centric attitude. Thus, what looks to us as spiritual are phenomena measured mainly along the dimension of information, while material phenomena are measured mainly along space-time. All phenomena are in the field of entropy-order.

The same which was said in regard to the religions and cultural evolution can be said in regard to the political regimes, which in ancient times were just another facet of the religio-cultural basis and in modern periods has replaced it. In other words the transition from a state which has an official religion, like Catholicism, to a secular state which has a basic constitution, like democracy or communism, expresses the same trend of movement against the force of segmentation, due to the pull of entropy. Thus, state religions in ancient times were serving two purposes, it fulfilled man's personal and instinctive desire to have a world view, and in the same time it was the cement which kept together the state as an wholesome structure. As stated already, in the early pagan world the conqueror imposed his gods on the conquered people. The Roman empire adopted another policy, it allowed the subservient states to keep their own gods, but insisted that the statue of the emperor will be worshipped as a divine figure. This symbolized the incorporation of the small state in the super state, namely the empire. Monotheistic Judaism did not fit into this design, and hence the many rebellions which characterized the period in which the Romans dominated Judea. Although the Jewish rebels were defeated, monotheism survived and spread all over the Roman empire until Constantine had to make Christanity the state religion in order to prevent internal strife, between the Christians and the pagans. Catholicism into which early Christanity evolved, adopted many of the beliefs and ceremonies of the pagans in order to be more easily accepted by these people. This was not tolerated by the Jews, nor by the Moslems who adopted monotheism a few centuries later. In the countries ruled by the Christian Catholics the Jews and Moslems were regarded as infidels, while in the Moslem empire the Christians and Jews were regarded as such. Hence, from earliest times the religious institution was an enterprise to work against the entropic forces tending to disintegrate a society. Where there were a multiplicity of religions under a particular jurisdiction, the power holders tended to seek religious homogeneity as a mean of protecting social-political stability. Thus, the Catholic kings drove from late medieval Spain the Jews and the Moors. They achieved homogeneity, but thereafter Spain was in continuous decline, despite its empire (*). A fact which tells us about the positive role of the pole of entropy in evolution, namely by its creating a multitude of mutations, of ideas as well as of forms. The variety of which guarantees against conservatism and decadence.

With all the progress made in certain parts of the world toward unity, one should not forget that at the background of the national political issue looms the national ethnic coherence of people. Yet these are pulled in the two opposing directions discussed above. One direction is the trend to form a nation and the other direction to form parties, divided according to the interest of socio-economic classes, or ethnic minorities, which try to take advantage of each other. In each party the persons involved aim to promote themselves and their ideas. Those controversial trends were solved already in the Greek Polis or city state by the democratic system which gave the decisive posts to the representatives of the majority of the people (In the Greek Polis it did not include slaves). At that time, most states were consolidated by a hierarchic governmental system, at the head of which stood a king-priest who was the representative of God. In general, in ancient times, the government by a monarch at the head of the state or empire, having full authority to decide the fate of his nation, was self evident. To question the monarch's absolute authority, not to say to defy it, evoked the most harsh punishment. The same was in regard to religion; the reign over the spiritual matters was by an autocratic potentate regarded as the representative of god on earth. Absolute obedience to his decisions was the basic law; any confutation induced punishment. At a certain stage during the evolution of the modern state, the two governing autocrats divided power between them. The king or noble had the full dominion on the body of his subject, while the religious master enslaved his spirit. As late as the seventeenth century in Western Europe, political power rested on the premise *Ejus Regio; ejus relligio,* which translates roughly, 'He who has the political power determines the religion of the subjects' (*). This lasted until the Thirty Years War in Europe (1618–1648) which started as a war between the Catholic and Protestant religions, and finished as a war between nations. This war decided in general lines the present division of Europe into states. Nationalism, namely the loyalty to the national state replaced the loyalty to the religion, although some emperors, like the Russian Tzar, and the Austro-Hungarian Kaizer tried to play with the two cards. The American Revolution (1775) and later the French revolution (1789) estranged, expressively, religion from government and education. However, while the French had ethnic and national identity as a bond, the United States of America had to find the way in which the abstract principles of its constitution will play the same role that religion once played (and still plays in traditional communities), and nationalism plays in most countries.

As already said, it is out of the scope of this book to discuss the history and describe the evolution of the political and religious systems. For this purpose, more than one book, not to say chapters, are needed. In the present discussion, I would only like to accentuate the thesis that the principles of the evolution of human societies is similar to that found in the evolution of the bio-world. In both, one finds on the one hand the pull towards disorganization, and on the other the pull towards the formation of larger and thus stronger societies. In the case of the human society, the strength desired is in the material as well as the spiritual domains, which reflect the different dimensions of STI. The more primitive the society, the more is the power of material affinities, i.e. related mainly to space-time dimensions. The more evolved the society is, the more its power will be pronounced by the evolution of the intelligence of the society, namely advancement along the dimension of information. This conflict between separatism and cosmopolitanism is the background to the political progress and retreat on the international scale, while the conflict between parties, minorities and classes, is the background of the arrow towards entropy on the national scale.

Yet, as already mentioned, if one examines the history of mankind from its prehistoric beginning, one may say that although the general pull is towards more diversity, the main arrow points towards bigger and more ordered societies, and even more democracy, expressing a higher level of agreement between nations and individuals. This expresses the continuation of the general arrow of the evolution of the universe, from chaos towards more order.

An interesting aspect of the arrow of evolution, is revealed by man's tools. While the diversification in the animal world was according to the changing habitat, (thus fish developed lungs and legs, reptiles wings and mammals brains) the diversification of the Homo-sapiens seems to be by developing instruments, cars, airplanes, rockets and computers. The more sophisticated the tools, the more they are advanced on the dimension of information. Also the means, tools and systems by which information was transferred evolved. Before man could write he could send messages by drumming on a hollow tree trunk, or by smoke. Later on the runners, carrying written messages played an important role in the ability of rulers to administer their countries and empires. The communication system in the Persian empire was based on horsemen, as well as on fire signals transmitted from the top of artificially built mounds. The Roman Empire had an efficient system of roads, on which chariots and horseman carrying dispatches could move rapidly, as well as armies and their supplies. The international post system, and later the telegraph and telephone systems, not to speak on the radio and TV have shortened distances, and create a bridge between communities which were alienated by geographical as well as cultural distance.

All these inventions brought on one hand the possibility of better communication and thus better organization. On the other hand, it enables the negative forces, namely those which strive to disorganize the national and multi-national organization, to have enough power to enforce their will and regime on other societies. This conflict between liberalism and fanaticism, between cosmopolitanism and separatism, will undoubtedly continue forever, as the two forces towards entropy and negative-entropy are self-complimentary. The result of these struggles are, as in other phenomena in nature, a wave pattern of ups and downs, summits and depressions.

If the reader agrees with my general conclusion that the main arrow of evolution of mankind points towards an increase in order, organization and intelligence, he should also agree that the intelligent forecast regarding the social structure of mankind is a pluralistic, international organization, liberal and intelligent, ruled by tolerant people who were chosen in a democratic way, representing the different nations of the world, this vision is in spite of all the short-term drawbacks of strife and local wars.

To the reader who is worried that such a world may prove to be a too dull place to live in, I can point out the tremendous challenges that intelligent humanity still faces, from the improvement of the welfare of the underdeveloped countries, to correcting and avoiding the evils that overdeveloped countries have inflicted on the natural environment, the looming calamity of climate change due to the Greenhouse Effect, not to speak of the problem of supplying more food and water to an ever increasing population. If there is still a young man to whom these challenges are not enough, I will suggest to him to look upwards to the skies, on a nice starry night (trusting he does it in a place not shrouded by smog). Training his vision for a short while, he will be able to see the space above him, dotted by the multitude of stars, three dimensionally; the smaller dimmer stars will appear to be further away than the larger brighter stars. Once he succeeds seeing this he will grasp the depth of space. At this instant he can say to himself: as there is no limit to the sky there is no limit to the will of man to progress.

7 The information dimension in retrospect

Contemporary cosmology claimed to demonstrate that the dimensions of space and time somehow emerged from the fireball of the Big Bang. Issar suggests that the Information Dimension is a cosmological dimension intrinsic to space-time. It is man who grasps it and builds his conceptual models by arranging the information quanta against the gradients of the field of entropy.

As David Bohm has reminded us, the word fact comes from the Latin *facere*, to make. It is to that construction that I now turn. All living organisms receive signals from their environment. Man is pre-eminent and perhaps unique in the capacity to translate signals into language, and thus to understand his environment and to develop projects to control or remake it. Man confronts raw data against a background of 'noise'. For data to become constituents of information, it must ordered. The patterns of order, or at least the most important ones, are the following:

1 topological
2 temporal
3 taxonomic
4 correlative
5 causal
6 numerical (including mathematics)

The reader will note perhaps that the above list is suggestive of the Kantian categories. But here they are considered not as the conditions for experience, but the results thereof. Now a word about each of the categories. By topological we refer to the distribution of objects in space (this is the sense of the Greek word *topos,* which means place). It is obvious that without this capacity our remote ancestors would never have survived. The temporal sense emerged at an unknown period, but without the capacity to order events in some quantitative sense or their succession in time, survival would be in doubt. With the earliest glimmers of settlement, our ancestors were aware of the cycles of day and night, the flux of the seasons, the time for planting, the time for reaping, etc. The nature of time has puzzled theologians, philosophers, and scientists throughout history. Thus it has been and remains an important segment on the information dimension. In historical times we have gone from the invention of calendars to the discovery of biological clocks which apparently exist in all living organisms. The category, taxonomic, has been somewhat neglected in the history of ideas. But if Issar's thesis is accepted, its importance becomes obvious.

'Because some things are similar, science is possible. Because some things are different science is necessary'. There is an obvious link between the following processes: observe, name, sort, classify and the development of language itself. The abstracting capacity of the human mind was stimulated by the taxonomic activity. In its earliest operations it was vital to species survival. Consider only the difference between a poisonous plant and a nutritional one. A thousand generations later we will have the Mendeleev Table and the Linnean system of the phylla, genus, species ordering. The Sumerians were the first people who made an inventory of the objects in their environment, particularly the flora and fauna. Their method was classifying in terms of the linguistic structure of the noun. This was scientifically futile, but it indicated their belief in an underlying order in nature. Here, also, was created the first bilingual dictionary: Akkadian-Sumerian. This permitted, for the first time, the exchange of information between peoples of diverse ethnic origin. It is an irony of history that the legend of the Tower of Babel involved these peoples.

Mathematicians will classify the numbers, the functions, and eventually the geometries. In contemporary times elementary particles have been subjected to a rigorous and fruitful taxonomy. Good taxonomies are more than neatly classified objects or ideas. They always suggest an order in nature or in human affairs and suggest to the inquiring mind underlying dynamics. It may be of interest to note here that the classification of written literature was begun by Callimachus, a librarian in the great library of Alexandria. Later we will have the Dewey Decimal system, the system of the Library of Congress, and finally, the ISBN, the international system which permits librarians all over the world to know from a series of numbers the general content of a printed book.

The correlative category includes most statistical data or forms of explanation. Quite often, particularly in the early stages in the development of a discipline, correlations are found by investigators and these lead usually to a search for a causal function. The history of medicine could not be written without taking this into account.

Ever since Aristotle, the search for causes has been the great goal of the inquiring mind. In our day the term has been stripped of its intimation of determinism and still remains the link between data, information, and knowledge.

We are not certain when the number sense emerged and there is obviously a great gap between counting, ordering and what is implied by the term mathematics. All that we want to point out here is that ever since its beginning in the Fertile Crescent, perhaps 3,000 B.C., most mathematics has been preserved and has been available across space and time to inquiring scholars. In Issar's sense it should be thought of as a separate language, useful and sometimes mandatory for progress along the dimension of information. It is obvious that the Greeks derived some mathematics from their Egyptian and Babylonian predecessors. But it was they who had the glory of creating a formal logical discipline from what was essentially the empirical knowledge of their teachers. Thereafter the scientists of any age have found ready at hand the mathematics requisite for their work. For example, the mathematics of Archimedes, Euclid, and Apollonius was sufficient to underpin the work of Galileo, Kepler, and Descartes. After the invention of the infinitesimal calculus by Newton and Leibniz, the vocabulary of mathematics, purged of ambiguities imposed by common language, expanded exponentially. In the nineteenth century mathematicians developed non-Euclidean geometry, matrix algebra, the calculus of variations, the Hamiltonian equations — all of which will be available for the revolutions we associate with relativity theory and quantum mechanics. As mentioned before, this new language and its notation became a universal resource.

The above schema in operation may be best explained by a brief glance at the history of science. I shall start with the scientific revolution of the seventeenth century.

The path from Copernicus to Newton is best demonstrated in the most economical fashion by the following:

1 Copernican heliocentrism (topological)

2 Galilean kinematics for freely falling bodies:

$$s = \frac{gt^2}{2}$$

3 Descartes postulation of conservation of momentum which may be written:

$$\frac{d(mv)}{dt} = 0$$

4 Kepler's laws:

a planetary orbits are elliptical, with the sun at one focus

b the radius vector sweeps out equal areas in equal times

c the relation of mean distance from sun to orbital time is:

$$T^2 = kR^3$$

5 Huyghen's law for centrifugal force which may be written:

$$F_C = \frac{mv^2}{r}$$

6 Newton's law of gravitation, a knowledge set which subsumes all of the above.

$$F_g = G\frac{m \cdot m'}{r^2}$$

It is to be noted here that this is a progression from a topological description to a causal law. Similar intellectual dramas will be played out in most branches of physics and chemistry.

It is to be noted that all of the mathematics that went into the above could be carried out using the techniques inherited from the Greeks. Newton used his fluxions to prove things for himself.

It is to be noted that after the seventeenth century, physicists and astronomers will find ready at hand all the mathematics they will need. That is why mathematics should be thought of as a knowledge set, a set constantly expanding through interaction with investigators of the external world. What has amazed many of the most skillful appliers of mathematics is that this symbolic world is sufficiently rich to permit the most complex structures and processes to be put into a one-to-one correspondence with mathematical symbols. Examples of mathematical structures created without any impetus for utility are:

1 Non-Euclidean geometry,

2 Non-commutative algebra,

3 Boolean algebra,

4 Matrix algebra,

5 Theory of complex variables.

By now it is evident that these were the analytical tools with which subatomic spaces and processes were explored and expanding universes, black holes, and neutron stars were predicted.

The foregoing sketch will culminate in the great Newtonian synthesis. It illustrates reasonably well how data and information culminate in knowledge. The key term here is synthesis. The law of universal gravitation unified the mechanics of heaven and earth. For the next two centuries it will be the supreme paradigm, the model for the investigation of many other diverse phenomena. It enhanced respect for human reason, and since it was carried out mainly by mathematicians, it established permanently the prestige of that discipline. In the next century it will lead Immanuel Kant, the first philosopher who mastered the science of his age, to assert that there was as much certainty in science as there was mathematics.

In the next century as investigators probed the phenomena of heat, electricity, magnetism, and light, we will find the same sequence from data to information to knowledge. The empirical laws of Coulomb, Ohm, and Ampere will lead to the grand synthesis of Maxwell, unifying the laws of electricity, magnetism, and light. Also, the empirical gas laws starting with Boyle, Charles, and others will culminate in the synthesis associated with the names of Maxwell and Boltzmann.

Issar's thesis is also well illustrated if we look at other human aspects of the scientific revolution. Surely the distribution of intelligence was not greater before the seventeenth century than during it or afterwards. Yet the most extraordinary thing about the history of science is that after the seventeenth century the process of developing science is vastly accelerated. It is my suggestion that this is to be explained first of all by the fact that in the seventeenth century, scientific academies were established, and, with the scientific academies, the scientific journal. And since there was a fairly well developed postal system by the seventeenth century, the regular appearance of journals to which all scholars were invited to contribute permitted the focus of human intelligence upon the same set of problems, in the same way that a magnifying glass concentrates the rays of the sun. So the academies with their journals created an information network that permitted problems to be isolated, discussed and eventually solved. This process of course has continued on to our own day. The other great contribution of the seventeenth century which contributed to the rate of acceleration was the development of the instruments of science. It is an extraordinary fact that this seminal achievement has been given very little attention. However, it is perfectly clear that a scientific instrument represents the codification of a great deal of science in its very structure, and increases the range through which the scientific mind can probe the cosmos The microscope, the telescope, the pendulum clock, the barometer, the thermometer, all permit the scientist to enhance, to amplify the capacities which he has in virtue of his physical-biological being, his five senses. The telescope gives to the astronomer a gods-eye capacity of vision towards the infinitely large. The microscope permits him to uncover and analyze and explore the world of infinitely small. Furthermore, once the first prototype of such an instrument has been created, it begins to evolve; but the evolution is 'Larmarckian', acquired characteristics are passed on to descendants, and one goes in a relatively short period of time against the clock of geological history, in ten generations, from Galileo's little hand-held and hand-made telescope to the 200-inch telescope on Mount Palomar in California and to the great array of radiotelescopes that now dot our planet and permit the extraction of information from the most distant galaxies. Very rapidly the scientists moved from visible light straight up the spectrum of electromagnetic radiation, infrared, ultraviolet, gamma rays, etc., bringing the entire information containing radiation within the scope of human intelligence. Here should be noted the non-linearity of this kind of progress. When the camera was married to the spectroscope, the capacity of analyzing the life and death of stars was immediately at hand. When the electronic beam was focused by a magnetic field, one came very close to understanding the structure of cells. When the X-ray was united with other laboratory devices, and put in conjunction with the science of crystallography, the structure of molecules became available. Molecular biology, which is the cutting edge of the current scientific revolution, became possible. One could sum up the foregoing by noting that with the formation of academies of science and the journals of science, a community emerged that crossed national boundaries. It was the first community that was self-correcting. Members within this community, wherever they were located in space or time, could operate at the same point on the dimension of information.

It should not be assumed that with these achievements, the scientific community obtained absolute autonomy. Newton himself devoted perhaps two-thirds of his working life to the study of biblical chronology, alchemy, and other non-scientific texts. He reintroduced the atoms of Democritus, purged of their association with atheism by Pierre Gassendi. But he ascribed their existence to divine creation and he asserted that his absolute space was the sensorium of God. Probably the first modern scientist, if we equate modernity with disassociation from theological, political, or philosophical commitment was Laplace. When Laplace's great work *System of the World,* was given to the Emperor Napoleon, who by the way was the first modern ruler who understood the nature of science and mathematics. Napoleon read it and meeting Laplace in the corridors of the palace said to him, "Monsieur I have read your work. It is a great work, but you have not mentioned God." To which Laplace replied, "Sire, I had no need of such an hypothesis."

As counterpoint to the ideas of Laplace we may note that the great Swiss mathematician, Leonard Euler, contemplating the equation

$$e^{i\pi} + 1 = 0$$

presented this to the famous French materialist physicist D'Alembert. He repeated the equation (which unites the exponential function, the trigonometric function, and complex variables) and then asserted boldly, "Therefore the good God exists." Apparently D'Alembert was left speechless! Euler's argument was philosophically similar to the nineteenth century argument based on the 'fitness' of biological structures. The point of all of this is that we can understand more clearly the great achievements of the seventeenth century if we never forget that these intellectual works were accomplished in a period of great political and social upheaval where there was literally a hurricane of prejudice derived from ancient belief systems sweeping Europe. The political passions in all cases were matched by the theological passions also. Nonetheless, the heavens yielded up their secrets and these were embodied in the differential equations of the new calculus.

For all the grandeur of its accomplishments, the community of scientists who made the scientific revolution in the seventeenth century operated under a number of constrictions, some self-imposed, and others the result of the historical ambiance. The important elements of the latter may be summarized as follows:

In the sixteenth century three charismatic men each endowed with a powerful intellect and iron will cast long and sinister shadows over the age to come. They were Niccolo Machiavelli 1459–1527, Ignatius Loyola 1491–1556, and Martin Luther 1483–1546. The Florentine, Niccolo Machiavelli, in his study of statecraft, severed the reality of politics from all moral discourse and considerations of ethics. The German, Martin Luther, Augustinian monk, shattered the unity of Christianity, broke the monopoly of the Roman church over the Christian conscience, but delivered his followers, bound in blind obedience, to the rule of the princes. Ignatius Loyola, the Spaniard, was the moving spirit of the counter-reformation and introduced into intellectual discourse the ruthlessness of war to the end. Albeit the song 'Onward Christian Soldiers, Marching as to War,' became a popular ditty only in the nineteenth century, its beginnings are to be found in the work and writings of the Spanish founder of the Jesuit order. These considerations, grim though they may be, are relevant to Issar's main thesis. The unity of the Christian world, once shattered, was never put back together. When the German peasants, inspired by religious ideas, rose in rebellion against feudal oppression, Martin Luther, the theological rebel, preached a war of extermination against them. In so doing, he separated theology from social justice. The work of the three men taken together will affect not only the nature of information and knowledge as it will evolve in the great century of the scientific revolution, it will also create those fissures in our general culture which haunt contemporary man. Martin Luther will also introduce into the main stream of Protestantism the bacillus of medieval antisemitism, and the followers of his counterpart in Geneva, John Calvin, will link commercial success, no matter by what means it was attained, to the benediction of divine providence. Again, these facts of theological history are cited because they form the background within which the new academies of science were emerging. Albeit the legacy of these power theoreticians was the Thirty Years War, the more important legacy was that there was removed from the study of the human condition by the emerging social sciences any concern with the ancient notions of justice and compassion which were to be found in the works of Plato and which carried over, albeit in a transformed manner into some of the social tenets of early Christianity. Thus it is no accident that pioneers in the social sciences such as the Englishman, Thomas Hobbes, and his successor, the gentle John Locke, concentrated on the mechanics of government, the separation of powers, the nature of the state. Those who were powerless were not studied. The histories that were compiled in the seventeenth and eighteenth centuries ignored the artisans, the craftsmen, and the peasants upon whose labor the whole structure of civilization stood. Luther also denounced Copernicus as a fool who had overturned scripture. The German humanists, very much under the influence of the new theological tendencies, were also hostile to the emerging sciences, suspicious of its inductive and analytical methods, ignorant of the mathematics which underpinned it. The old universities, apart from their continued teaching of mathematics and medicine ignored the new sciences, and it was well into the nineteenth century before there will be chairs in physics and chemistry in places such as Cambridge, Oxford, the Sorbonne, and other ancient seats of learning. On Issar's information dimension the solitary scientists journeyed almost alone, their journals of little significance to the poets and the lawyers and the power movers. This is also the epoch, particularly after the end of the Thirty Years War when those European peoples facing the Atlantic hurled themselves with ruthless fury upon the Americas, Africa and the coasts of Asia. This was also the period in which the ships crossing the Atlantic had as their most precious cargo black slaves purchased in Africa to be sold at auction in North and South America. This will lead Montesquieu in the eighteenth century to say that the Europeans did not consider the Negroes to be human, for if they did, they could not consider themselves to be Christians. And what about the Incas, the Mayas, the Aztecs, the Iroquois, the Hurons, the Comanches?

It is only in the light of the above historical sketch that we can understand the far-reaching import of two rather obscure documents from the seventeenth century. The first is Hook's preamble to the charter of the Royal Society.

> The business of the Royal Society is: To improve the knowledge of natural things, and all useful Arts, Manufactures, Mechanic practices, Engynes, and Inventions by Experiement — (not meddling with Divinity, Metaphysics, Morals, Politics, Grammar, Rhetorick, or Logicks).

The second is from Rene Descartes:

> If, in place of the speculative philosophy taught in the schools, one could find a practical one, by which, knowing the force and the action of fire, the air, and the stars, and those of all the other bodies which surround us, as distinctly as we know the crafts of our artisans, we could use them in the same way, where appro-

priate and thus make ourselves masters and possessors of nature. (Eaton, 1955)

One may conclude from looking at these two documents conjointly that the study of nature has been fatefully severed from the study of man; that the community of scientists will not have as their primary concern the moral consequences of what is done with their knowledge. Forgotten is the voice from the Renaissance, that of François Rabelais: "Science without conscience is but the ruin of the soul."

Furthermore, all of the ancient emotions and intuitions concerning the 'sacredness' of nature will be ignored. The old Greeks would have found the phrase 'make ourselves masters and possessors of nature' the kind of hubris or arrogance that the gods would be sure to punish. It is not unreasonable to believe that most of the ecological and environmental disasters looming on our horizon have their origin here.

There was also a certain parochialism in the scientific community's concern with or understanding of non-Western European societies. The Europeans had happily borrowed much high technology from China: paper, movable type, ceramics, porcelain, the compass, the controllable rudder, and that mixed blessing — gunpowder. They were, however, indifferent to the Taoist philosophy which was profoundly concerned with man's place in nature and commanded that man live in harmony with nature.

The style of scientific communication of the future has its origin here. Eliminated will be the agony and ecstasy of discovery that we find in Kepler and Galileo. The scientific paper and monograph will be written stripped of all the human quality that went into its making.

Among the great pioneers, Leibniz alone had a sense of history. He hoped for a communication between East and West, and even suggested to the Russian Czar, Peter the Great, that Russia should constitute such a bridge. It was also Leibniz who noticed that the disputes between theologians and philosophers often turned on the ambiguity of the terminology in use. He hoped to eliminate this by translating all such propositions into a numerical, algebraic form, his universal characteristic. He would say to the angry debaters, "Stop shouting. Sit down. Let us calculate!" (Weiner, 1951). His contemporary, Spinoza, tried to derive an absolute ethical system in the manner of Euclid. He stated his ideas in terms of axioms and theorems, ending each argument with the Euclidian Q.E.D. what was to be demonstrated. Since Spinoza derived the entire corpus from a theory of deity, his noble effort lacked specificity and utility.

Spinoza looked backward to age of Aquinas. Leibniz looked forward to the age of Boolean algebra, the computer, and expert systems. We might note in passing that it was Leibniz who improved on Pascal's desk calculator, enabling it to use the four arithmetic operations.

A moment's contemplation will convince us that art, all of the arts, convey information to the human observer or participant. The relation between science and art is a disputed terrain. I am concerned here not with C.P. Snow's problem of 'the two cultures'. The reader will recall that Snow (1963) juxtaposed the scholar who understood the second law of thermodynamics and the humanist who was an expert in interpreting Hamlet. According to Snow they had nothing to say to each other. I regard this as a contingent failure of higher education, telling us nothing about how Shakespeare and Boltzmann communicate with us.

There is beauty in art and in science. This was most eloquently stated by the last of the universal mathematicians, Henri Poincarè in his *Science and Method* (1952), he stated that simplicity as well as grandeur can be carriers of beauty. We seek simplicity in the majestic course of the stars, and also in that minuscule world revealed by the microscope. What is most illuminating in the brief essay by Poincrè is his linkage of the beautiful and the useful. We could expand this idea to find beauty in that child of science, technology. Poincrè found this in architecture.

It was Thomas Browne, a contemporary of Newton, who said, "Architecture is frozen music."

It is clear that information has flowed from the artist to the community and that peculiar kind of unknown feedback back to the artist. In great ages of art this is clearer than in our own somewhat fragmented epoch. It is perfectly obvious that if we look at the Athenian polis or any of the Greek city-states we can see a harmony of all of the parts. We can see this also in the high Middle Ages. We can see it in Renaissance Florence. We can see it in Elizabethan England. At what point human culture became so fragmented that these unities were lost we do not know.

Some of the deeper implications of Issar's information dimension can be glimpsed by comparing mathematics and music. The first song is probably as old as the first spoken sentence and both are lost in the mists of time. The remnants of crude musical instruments have been found at paleolithic sites. The first conservatory was probably a tree full of singing birds. Egyptian temple paintings ca. 2,600 B.C. depict reed and stringed instruments. The pipes of Pan and the lute of Orpheus belong to the age of the water clock and the sun dial. Musical notation and mathematical notation evolved together towards ever-increasing orders of complexity and information carrying capacity.

As a footnote to our calling attention to the unity of mathematics and music, we might take a look at a page of sheet music with its five bar staff, the individual notes, and all of the other bits of symbolism that indicate tempo and tone and timbre, etc., the sharps and the flats and the notation of andante non tropo, pianissimo, fortissimo, etc. which carry instructions, information, to the performing musician. What we have here is an amplification of the information contained in each individual set of notes. In a similar way, without stretching the point too far, we can look at a series of equations. For example, if one writes Y = function of X, and then puts an integral sign before the function, the second set of symbols contain more information. And then if one adds the upper and lower limits of integration, the information is again amplified. In the same way the musical score carries information to the individual musician and to the community of musicians performing a certain piece under the baton of a conductor. And to understand perhaps most distinctly the role of cybernetics in information flows, merely watch a dress rehearsal of a symphonic orchestra and the way in which a master conductor with a motion of a wrist or the raise of an eyebrow brings, say, the first violins into a closer tempo or detects the slightest loss of pitch by the bassoons.

The historical record shows that the variety and precision of musical instruments evolved parallel with the instruments of science. The Stradivarius violins are coeval with the microscope and telescope. It was probably coincidental that the first second order partial differential equation in physics grew out of the study of the vibrating string of a violin. The assembly of one hundred instruments for a symphonic orchestra come into being at roughly the same time as the spread of instruments into all of the domains of scientific investigation. This is equivalent to observing that the flow of scientific information is concomitant with the flow of aesthetic information. Unfortunately the latter has not been studied with the same detail as the history of science and the history of technology, but it is perfectly clear that the artist is making a statement about the world and also about the human soul. Perhaps this is best indicated by observing what somebody said (exactly who I have forgotten) that music is the soul counting without knowing that it is counting. To the trained eye, there is always a peculiar fit between the art and architecture of an age and its science. Historians have puzzled over this because they have no coherent explanation. They have invented the term zeitgeist, the German term which translates as spirit of the time, or climate of opinion. How this is spread so that it becomes part of the psyche of a community we simply do not know.

While pondering this problem of music and science, my son sent me as a gift an extraordinary book entitled *Art and Physics* by Leonard Shlain (1991). Because his theory converges on that of Issar, I wish to examine it in depth.

He starts by asserting that during the Renaissance 'Literacy in both the printed word and music brought about the rise in the importance of the hand and the eye at the expense of the voice and the ear.' What he has in mind here, of course, is the development of written notation for music. Before this period the musical corpus was committed to memory and could be lost. Now there was the symbolic notation — a symbolism for capturing sound waves as potent in its way as the development of mathematical notation in the seventeenth century. As he says, music and speech became visible. What is more important, the printed word and the printed sheet music became transportable. Geographical, political frontiers became meaningless. The maritime powers in this same period were thrusting their power, their culture into the newly discovered continent. We see here the remote beginnings of a global civilization whose style and content would be set in the west. The written notation permitted a deeper analysis of music, the discovery of the principles of harmony, etc. As Shlain summarizes it, advances in musical technique, like perspective in art and the Copernican system in science allowed music to be considered 'a three dimensional aural geometry that was structured by the flow of time.'

The acceptance of new art forms is not always smooth though we know of no martyrs in painting, music, or literature. It is also the case that there were riots when musicians presented work that broke with the traditional canon. The first impressionists were thought of as beasts. But by and large it would appear that innovation of the arts has been less a stormy process than that of science.

All cultures have a trinity of symbols that express the highest of human yearning: the true, the beautiful, the good. In western culture, the true has become associated with science, the beautiful with art, the good with ethics. Throughout recorded history these three have often interpenetrated each other. For purposes of Issar's thesis, I wish to look at ethics in isolation.

The records of moral discourse go back to the ancient Egyptians. With them we find the idea of conscience, the concept of individual responsibility for action, the idea of judgment, and an obsession with immortality and eternity. Many of the moral precepts of the

Egyptians, commingled with some from the Babylonian, were put by the Hebrews in the Old Testament. Since those earliest of times, ethical precepts have been carried across time and space by theology and codes of law. Both of these media have possessed immense inertia and appear in cultures radically different from the place of origin. For example, many of the harsh legal mandates of contemporary Islamic law were found already in the code of Hammurabi, the Babylonian, circa 1800 B.C. During the seventh and sixth centuries B.C., there was an unexplainable fluorescence of the religious and philosophical spirit: Buddhism in India, Confucianism and Taoism in China, Zoroasterism in Iran, the pre-Socratics within the Hellenic world.

The passage from religious and poetical moral discourse to what we would recognize as elements of contemporary ethical insight begins in Greece with the Sophists. This is beautifully expressed by the scholar, Arnold Hauser (1957), in his masterwork *The Social History of Art.*

To bring the discussion of ethics as an information system into some historical context I wish to proceed from mention of the ancient East and Near East and look briefly at the roots of our contemporary discourse about ethics. I find these, as have so many others before me, in the Hellenic world. I might say that I grew up (in my school days it is) with Socrates, Plato and Aristotle. Only later did I encounter scholarly discussions of the sophists. The great masterwork of Arnold Hauser, informs us of the radical break that these teachers made from aristocratic tradition that goes back to pindar and beyond. The sophists broke with the shadowy notion of virtue being embedded in inheritance and stimulated by physical training. They were the first who taught that character could be shaped by education, by learning. That this has contemporary echo in American politics should be obvious at all. As Hauser put it, 'they initiated the history of rationalism with its criticism of dogmas, myths'. They began the tradition, thereafter uninterrupted to this day, that all truths are historically conditioned. As Hauser puts it 'their teaching paved the way for all subsequent endeavor in the field of humanistic enlightenment'. He also notes 'their experience of ancient capitalism aroused the same reactions in them as the experience of modern capitalism does in their successors.'

We should note that the Mosaic Laws, like most legal codes, enumerate a set of prohibitions. With the New Testament there is a significant shift in emphasis. The content of moral behavior is made specific: do unto others as you would have them do unto you. Love thy neighbor as thyself. Forgive us our transgressions and we forgive those who transgress against us.

Unfortunately these admonitions were destined not to apply (in practice) to infidels, heretics, schismatic and, much later on, to the 'lesser breeds without the law'.

Furthermore the Christian fathers made a fateful division within the domain of moral action: render unto Caesar what is Caesar's and unto God what is God's. The old Greeks were aware of this tension, and it occurs more than once in their tragic dramas, like Antigone, etc. (Murray and Rogers, 1943).

In 800 A.D., the Pope crowned Charlemagne as Holy Roman Emperor. Approximately 1,000 years later, Napoleon Bonaparte, having wiped out the remnants of the Holy Roman Empire, kneeling in front of the Pope, will put the crown on his own head, declaring himself Emperor, not of France, but of the French. In that thousand year period, the representatives of God and those of Caesar spilled oceans of blood in the quest for supremacy.

Looked at in another way, we can say that we move from the era of faith, hope and charity to that of liberty, equality, fraternity. Put another way, from the contemplation of the moral universe to political action aimed at creating a more perfect secular human world.

The passion to ascribe great human achievements to the intervention of gods or God did not end with Aeschylus. It will recur throughout the history of the last two thousand years.

Only a few generations separate the publication of Newton's *Principia* and the publication by Adam Smith of his *Inquiry Into the Wealth of Nations*. In that interval the new figurehead appeared that would soon take center stage, the engineer. His roots go back to the military engineers such as Archimedes and the Roman engineers who had built the great roads and aqueducts of the Roman empire, to the highly skilled craftsmen who had built the imperial roads of ancient Persia and of Rome. Now they appear as civil engineers, mechanical engineers, etc. First they are the choreographers of coal and water and steam. Unfortunately they take over from their scientific predecessors that same indifference to the ethical consequences of their work that is embodied in the preamble to the Royal Society quoted above. They controlled the new power of steam and arranged the pulleys and drives and governors that made the industrial revolution. They are above all practical men and their supreme value is efficiency. And it should be noted that the first slag heaps and the first belching smoke over the pleasant landscapes of England are coeval with the erection of the first industrial slums. In the clamor of machinery, the voices of

Renaissance humanism were forgotten. Rabelais, as noted above, had said that science without conscience was the ruin of the soul. Now this could be updated to say that industrialism without conscience was the ruin not only of the soul but of society, and ultimately, of the planet. Well into the nineteenth century, little girls, six to eight years of age, three-quarters naked, crawled into narrow coal seams to hand lumps of coal to half-naked soot-covered men. It was not until 1924 that the Supreme Court of the United States of America upheld the constitutionality of child labor laws. For centuries the churches had intoned the words of Christ 'Suffer little children to come unto me'. And that most moral voice of the Renaissance, William Shakespeare, had put into the mouth of the woman, Portia, the words:

> The quality of mercy is not strain'd, —
> It droppeth as the gentle rain from heaven
> Upon the place beneath: it is twice blest, —
> It blesseth him that gives, and him that takes

It was neither engineer nor scientist nor politician who protested. It was the poets. They saw a world in which mercy counted for little, in which power over nature through machinery soon became the equivalent of the power of men over other men and the few over the many. The sacredness of nature had been replaced by the sacredness of property rights and contracts. It was Wordsworth who said:

> The world is too much with us; late and soon,
> Getting and spending, we lay waste our powers.
> Little we see in nature that is ours;
> We have given our hearts away, a sordid boon!

It was the poet William Blake who lamented the 'dark Satanic mills'. It was the poet Oliver Goldsmith in *The Deserted Village* who wrote the mournful lines, 'Ill fares the land, to hastening ills a prey, where wealth accumulates and men decay'.

As the nineteenth century advanced and as the new technological age established its hegemony over the entire world, the carriers of ethical messages became the great novelists of that epoch. One thinks immediately of Charles Dickens, Emile Zola, Flaubert, Dostoevsky, Tolstoy, Stendal. Not that the poets were silent, but as literacy expanded, and as paper and printing became cheaper, as public libraries were established, the novel carried the essential analysis of society. It should be noted that this was long before the social sciences as we know them now had been established in the great universities and had become part of popular knowledge. Closer to our own time we would note the works of Ignacio Silone, Andre Malraux, Thomas Mann, Maxim Gorky, and in their greater moments Theodore Dreiser, Ernest Hemingway, Upton Sinclair, Sinclair Lewis and John Steinbeck. It is a sad commentary on the history of ethical discourse that it was only in the third century of the history of the industrial revolution that courses in ethics became mandatory in the great business schools in the United States of America.

Having glanced briefly at the application in Issar's thesis to science, art, and ethics, it will now be appropriate to place his ideas in a global setting. In round numbers, we note that the biological evolution of our species reached the level permitting speech 150,000 years ago; writing emerged 5,000 years ago; printing 500 years ago. The first book with photographs appeared 150 years ago.

One hundred years after the completion of the work of Faraday, Maxwell, Hertz, Joseph Henry, and Crookes, telegraphy, the telephone, radio, the cinema, and television were in place globally. During the climax of World War II in 1944, the Mark IV computer was operational at Harvard University. Furthermore the V-1 and V-2 rockets had been launched by Germany against allied positions. This was the grim harbinger of the space age.

If we hold all of the above numbers in our minds, it immediately becomes clear that not only has there been a constant acceleration in human understanding and control of the natural world, but that the acceleration itself is accelerating. Furthermore, there is an unmistakable evidence of positive feedback — between what man does and what he becomes capable of doing. Such processes have a non-linearity about them.

We can now state a set of axioms concerning the accumulation of information and the evolution of information to knowledge:

1 The utility of information depends upon accessibility, understandability, and believability. If this circuit is broken at any point, the human value of information and knowledge for an individual or a community is nil.

2 Every tool, artifact, or machine that man makes represents a transfer of information from the human mind to the inanimate world.

3 The products of artists are governed by these same general principles, but we lack an appropriate language to describe them.

4 Neither Max Weber nor Karl Marx ever dreamed that the most important sociological division might be between those who were information rich and those who were information poor.

Probably no human activity mirrors more precisely the process of collecting raw data, ordering it into information sets, and then compounding it into knowledge than the art and science of the cartographer. Every culture has tried to map its vision of the world. The earliest maps survive in cuneiform tablets from ancient Sumer, probably from around the 3rd millennium B.C. Modern map making can be said to date from the great age of exploration and discovery that we associate with the voyages of Columbus, Magellan, Vasco da Gama, Thomas Cook, and others. Bit by bit, with the aid of sextant, chronometer, plumb line and theodolite, the shape of the continents emerged. The meandering paths of river basins were plotted. The words *terra incognita,* 'unknown land', and 'here there be monsters and dragons' were eliminated from the maps of the world. From Mercator on through the voyages of the nineteenth century the configuration of the land masses and the oceans and the mountain ranges of our planet were put in ordered fashion on the two-dimensional plane and later depicted on more elaborate mathematical projections. With the coming of plate tectonics, the complex history of the motion of the continents in space and time is beginning to emerge, and with it a deeper understanding of the distribution of all living organisms. The human imagination, however, has never been limited to the surface of this small planet. Already in the early seventeenth century, Galileo, using his tiny telescope, made the first map of the moon. In modern times, cartography has moved into all domains of science. The happy union of the computer, the spacecraft, the radar instrument, and instruments sensitive to X-rays, ultraviolet and infrared have permitted contemporary man to create maps of the most distant planets, to create maps of the cosmos, indicating the distribution of galaxies and clusters of galaxies. Probably the most important maps now being made are those that have to do with the geography of the cell — the human cell, the animal cell, the plant cell. This geography has been elucidated first by the optical microscope, the techniques of staining, and then brought down to angstrom units by the electron microscope. Now there is the mapping of the human genome, probably the most important cartographic expedition that our species has ever embarked on. Thus in the realm of the infinitely great, the cosmos, and the infinitely small, the cell, and down to the molecule, modern scientific instrumentation permits mapping. In a beautiful essay to which I am greatly indebted, Steven Hall, writing in the journal, *The Sciences*, of the New York Academy of Sciences, has taught us that the human process of map making, that is to say, the abstraction of certain themes from a mass of initially uncorrelated data, is in a certain way an exact analog of the method by which the human optical system organizes what is in the field of vision. The gestalt emerges through a complex process of data manipulation within that most magnificent of all computers, the human brain. It should also be noted that a sheet of music with its score and annotations is in a very precise sense also a map. The notes are arranged along longitude and latitude. And when the instructions on the score are followed by the musician, the music emerges along the dimension of time, and lives again in that most precise of all receptors, the human brain and its mind.

Since the time of Francis Bacon, what we might call 'technological optimists' have assumed that all advances in knowledge lead to an improvement in the human estate. This is, at best, a partial truth. Most of the elements in a brave new world sketched above will surely mature in the twenty-first century. Children now in kindergarten will face social tensions that our engineers, programmers and politicians have ignored.

In Japan there is already a factory where robots assemble robots. The theory of a computer that can design and assemble computers is past the design stage. All of this receives the mindless plaudits of a population trained to think primarily in terms of the acquisition of ever more consumer goods and televised entertainment. However, if the factory of the future, sterile and air-conditioned, has no human workers, what is to happen to the countless millions who are being rendered obsolete or marginalized?

In an incredible leap of the imagination Aristotle anticipated such a contingency. In his *Politics* he wrote:

> ... On the basis of these assumptions we may conclude that each article of property is an instrument for the purpose of life; that property in general is the sum of such instruments; that the slave is an animate article of property; and that subordinates, or servants, in general may be described as instruments which are prior to other instruments (i.e. animate instruments which must first be present before other, and inanimate, instruments can be used).
>
> There is only one condition on which we can imagine managers not needing subordinates, and masters not needing slaves. This condition would be that each (inanimate) instrument

> could do its own work, at the word of command or by intelligent anticipation, like the statues of Daedalus or the tripods made by Hephaestus, of which Homer relates that 'Of their own motion they entered the conclave of Gods on Olympus'. (Aristotle, 1943)

Aristotle imagined a shuttle that can weave of itself. Would that he could see the inside of a modern textile mill.

There is no question that until recently millions of clerks all over the world typed and filed information, a monotonous and mind-dulling project. The prophets of the new age justly say that anything the mind does automatically, a machine can and should do better. The question remains to what activities, to what exciting new functions will this countless army of drudges now turn.

The industrial revolution which mobilized the knowledge of all earlier epochs is only about ten generations old. Its movers and beneficiaries proclaimed from the beginning that the wealth of nations, guided by an invisible hand, would increase without limit. The new age will call some of these assumptions into question and ask in a new setting: 'To what end shall we earn our bread by the sweat of our brows?' In the new age it is probable that the cryptic dictum of Karl Marx will achieve some urgency and cogency: 'Hitherto the philosophers have interpreted the world. The problem is to change it.'

There is no question that the computer has already changed our world and will continue to do so in all areas of human activity. Already by the 1970s, computer experts estimated that using a laser in conjunction with a computer, 100 million bits of information could be stored on a square of photographic film about the size of a postage stamp. They amaze us by claiming that a library of 20,000 volumes can be stored on a piece of nickel no bigger than a book page. Theoretically with cryogenics all the information in all the libraries in the world could be stored in a container about the size of a human cranium.

This is indeed a marvel of engineering, but one is haunted by the question as to which human mind will be capable of understanding the stored wisdom of ages.

We may indeed marvel at human ingenuity. But what should be our response to the fact that in the United States, where most of this engineering was developed, there are twenty-seven million illiterates and each year, it is estimated, seven hundred thousand students graduate from high school who cannot read their diplomas.

It is one of the ironies, if not tragedies, of recent history that the industrial revolution gave an immense stimulus to the democratization of education. Industry and commerce required a reasonably literate work force. But as we moved into the epoch of automation and electronics, the work force in many parts of the world became increasingly 'de-skilled'. In the light of the foregoing it seems trivial to say that there has to be a redefinition of the significance of human existence. It will no longer do to define a man or a woman in terms of their function. A number of science fiction writers from H. G. Wells on have sketched Orwellian and apocalyptic nightmare scenarios which often turn on the power of small elites and the degradation of the many. We refer the reader to the set of axioms sketched above.

Let us look now at what kind of information is flowing through the global network. It is best to think of it as a spectrum in which trash is at one end and some marvelous knowledge at the other. In a recent book, *The Brain Has a Mind of Its Own,* Richard Restak, (1991) a physician, wrote:

> ... 'Without knowledge or approval, broadcasters determine when and how we're going to feel moral outrage or disgust or anger'. and that 'The visual media — movies, TV, advertising — have so far avoided doing something about the injurious effects on our brains' As a physician he is concerned with the harmful effects the endless stream of violence, sexual titillation, appeals to consumer greed and envy will produce. In the United States there have been innumerable governmental hearings, endless public debate, cottage industries set up in our universities and elsewhere — all concerned with pollution and Issar's information dimension.

What should be more perturbing is the recent creation of immensely power conglomerates controlling all avenues of information — book publishing, magazines, newspapers, films, television, musical records, etc. One need not be Orwellian to notice that such empires are not merely concerned with profits. Inevitably they become concerned with political power. A foretaste of all of this is actually present at the beginning of this century with the creation of the empire of William Randolph Hearst. As noted above, development of the information age may produce totally unpredicted and unpredictable social catastrophes.

At the other end of the spectrum we may note magnificent data bases of medical knowledge which can be made accessible to a physician anywhere in the world who has a telephone and it is entirely probable that even this instrument may be made unnecessary by satellites and new types of receivers.

Another glimpse into the twenty-first century and the new mode of communication in the scholarly world is provided by the work of the Institute for Scientific Information in Philadelphia, Pennsylvania.

Under the direction of Dr Eugene Garfield, this institute in its *Science Citation Index,* indexed 3,213 journals annually. These were published in 42 nations and in 21 languages. A similar service is provided for the social sciences and the humanities.

The technological optimists also tell us that the global communication network will create a global village. It should be pointed out, however, that the globalization of communication coincides in time with increased violence in nations and between them.

One does not doubt that information about the world might, under unknown circumstances, create a planetary consciousness. But again one must point out the difference between information and knowledge, and between knowledge and moral behavior.

In a wonderful book, *A History of News* by Mitchell Stephens (1988), we are informed that it took several years after the Manchus conquered China for the news to reach and be understood in the commercial capitals of the European world. When Napoleon I was defeated at Waterloo and sent off to St. Helena, this important event was not known in North America until three to four weeks later owing to the chance arrival of a ship from Europe. When Napoleon III was defeated and deposed at the end of the Franco-Prussian War in 1870, this could be printed in the *New York Herald Tribune* the next day (thanks to the Atlantic Cable). When John Fitzgerald Kennedy was assassinated in 1963, the whole world knew it in a matter of seconds, and the whole world could watch in real time the funeral procession. The question remains: Does information concerning an alien people engender, necessarily, respect, love, or the desire to live in peace? Probably never in modern history did two great nations know more about each other than England and Germany, yet they slaughtered each other to the point of exhaustion in what used to be called The Great War (1914–1918).

Probably all great eras of transition are full of contradictions. The old order is perishing and the new has yet to establish itself in human consciousness.

There is no question but that television that brought the Vietnam War to homes all over the world engendered through its imagery that moral revulsion that brought that long conflict to an end.

However, the recent war in the Persian Gulf was televised in real time and millions watched it with the same fascination with which children watch their moving targets in electronic arcades. Perhaps here one could conclude by updating Rabelais dictum quoted above: Technology without conscience is the ruin of the soul.

Information had always been a source of political and economic power. The development of the news services under the sponsorship of national governments as in England, France and Germany, did much to spread the orthodoxy of the imperial states. And one might add, parenthetically, that since public opinion became an important political factor, particularly after the French Revolution, the control of the flow of news was an important instrument of national and imperial control.

The not too distant ancestors of the modern worldwide television news reporting services were the international news gathering institutions such as Havas in France, Reuters in Britain, and Associated Press in the United States. These developed in the 1830s and 1840s and they themselves could become profitable enterprises only because of the previous widespread development of the daily newspaper which in turn depended upon high speed presses, cheap paper, and above all, a growing literate public.

The sinister use to which modern media of communication could be put was provided in Weimar Germany. There in a period of five years, from roughly 1928 to 1933, the Nazi movement, using all of the gadgetry of modern communication and transport, was able to turn a confused, divided and desperate population into a monstrous instrument of sinister power. Hitler used not only radio and the press, but also the airplane and the cinema. He used it with enormous skill or his cohorts did.

The remote ancestor of the Reuters electronic commercial news distributing empire were the Fuggers of Augsburg, Germany who for several centuries, from the 14th century on, dominated banking and commerce in central Europe. The success of the Fugger enterprises depended upon a series of what we would call newsletters that brought to the headquarters of this far-flung commercial empire news of merchandise movements and prices from all over Europe and later on from all over the world. It should also be noted that the rise to power of the Venetian republic depended also on the continuous flow of economic and commercial information from all of the trading centers of Europe. This enabled the artisans and merchants of Venice to quite often have decisive advantages over their competitors. By an irony of history, in the 1990s, the Congress of the United States is discussing turning over to the Central Intelligence Agency a primary responsibility for collecting commercial, economic and technological data from all over the world. The Doges of Venice, whether they be in heaven or hell, will smile at this.

A further illustration of the clarifying power of Issar's thesis is discovered if we examine the problem of understandability and believability of information flows in times of warfare. Ever since primitive tribes disputed for possession of feeding grounds, belligerents have wanted to know the intention and capabilities of both foes and friends. The Homeric epic and the Old Testament are full of such tales. With the rise of the modern nation-state, Intelligence and diplomatic services became highly professionalized. In our own time the second oldest profession has witnessed the intrusion of the most sophisticated instruments of modern science. Yet no gadgetry can replace human judgment. This is illustrated by two extraordinary episodes in World War II. The first had to do with the German preparation that became known and Operation Barbarossa — the plan to invade and destroy the Union of Soviet and Socialist Republics. The planning for this gigantic operation began probably as early as 1940, at the same time that some members of the German military and diplomatic establishment were still thinking of Operation Sea Lion, the invasion and conquest of the British Isles. Now it turned out that both the Soviet intelligence service and the British intelligence service early on derived some understanding of the shift in German strategy, and in 1940 and early 1941, the British secret intelligence service, through the intervention of Winston Churchill tried to convey this information to the Soviet high command, the politicians and marshals grouped around Joseph Stalin. The Soviet diplomats had, prior to the pact between Stalin and Hitler in August 1939, attempted to arrive at some kind of mutual defense pact with the British and the French. This is particularly pursued after the Munich agreement which opened up Eastern Europe to German expansion with the collapse and absorption of Czechoslovakia. Within the Soviet high command there were those who believed that the dynamics of German imperialism were such that sooner or later the Germans would attack the Soviet Union. There were on the other hand those who believed that the security of the USSR depended upon some kind of an agreement with the West. Hence there was controversy, both about the intentions of the Western powers and the intentions of the fascist Axis. Stalin and his immediate advisors were convinced that it was the policy of the British to save themselves by engaging the Soviet Union in armed conflict with Hitler's Europe. Because this belief became fixed and because it had a certain coherence, it was not a madman's fallacy. The whole policy of the British and the French prior to Munich had been to organize hostile groupings against the Soviet Union. And so it was not surprising that ultimately Stalin and his cohorts became convinced that the information coming from the British, even though it agreed with what was coming from the Soviet's own secret service, was tainted, that is to say, the western information was tainted. The net result of this inability to accept the information flow from Richard Sorge in Tokyo and the Red orchestra in Paris and Brussels was that the Germans obtained complete tactical and strategic surprise, a victory which cost the Russians perhaps 10 million additional casualties. Later in the war, when the British were able to read the most secret military communications of the Germans, they fed information relevant to the eastern front to a Soviet network operating in Switzerland. They thus guaranteed the believability of the information. The Soviet triumph during the great tank battles at Kursk were made possible by the advance warning reaching the Soviet high command.

The inverse of this process of not believing is carried by the second episode that I want to discuss, namely what became known as Operation Double-cross. When the Allies were preparing the assault against the armored shores of German occupied Europe, it became obvious that the success or failure of this operation would depend upon an element of surprise. Hence the Allies set about an elaborate deception, that is to say, they 'turned' a number of German espionage agents, who had been captured in Britain, fed them enough information to make them credible, created a phantom army in southern England to make the Germans believe that the assault when it came would be at Pas de Calais. Then they were so successful in feeding this kind of information to Hitler's high command that this command became utterly convinced that the main assault would be at Pas de Calais, that any other landing would be a feint. This explains in large measure, not only the success of the Normandy operation, but the relatively low casualties with which it was carried out. Hence, we see that false information, if crafted with sufficient skill, can appear in the mind of the recipient as reliable knowledge.

These episodes have a cautionary implication for the scientific community. Coherent theories about nature with their supporting experimental evidence and mathematical formalisms tend to freeze into orthodoxies, which tend to ignore or reject contrary data. After the enormous success of the germ theory of disease, as announced by Pasteur and his colleagues and immediate successors, it became quite difficult to introduce the notion of metabolic diseases, that is to say, diseases which we now know arise from the deficiency of vitamins or other essential metabolites. Finally, of course, pellagra, beri-beri and scurvy were cured by vitamins. Another example is the resistance to the idea of the reality of atoms. These were held by leading scholars as late as the end of the nineteenth century to be nothing but useful fictions. Finally it will be the analysis of Brownian movement which will give experimental rather than purely theoretical evidence for the reality of atoms. Another example of the resistance to new information concerns the effort to establish the ionization of electrolytes. Here the barrier was idea of the indivisibility of atoms following upon the acceptance of the theories of Dalton, Avogadro and others. In fact, one of the foremost scholars in this field, Swedish Svante Arrhenius almost had his doctoral dissertation rejected because he was describing what we now recognize as the ionization of salts. Arrhenius finally will receive the Nobel Prize in chemistry for his theories of the disassociation of substances in solution.

Even in mathematics, there have been occasions when totally new ideas have not been understood and hence ignored. The tragedy of the young genius, Evariste Galois is illustrative. On the evening before his death in a duel, he presented his seminal paper on the theory of groups to a distinguished group of French mathematicians. His ideas had no antecedents. His language was not understood. Fortunately his papers survived and became the starting point for a completely new domain of mathematical thought.

The scientific community as now organized would probably avoid the exclusionary action cited above. The immediate acceptance of the revolutionary theories of quantum mechanics and relativity theory attest to that. On what one might call the edges of science, there will always be conflict and doubt. The fairy tale that new scientific ideas are accepted because the old men of orthodoxy die out is both false and insulting. Scientists not only debate among themselves; they conduct a continual interrogation of nature. There is never a dearth of new evidence. The global structure of the scientific community guarantees this. Experimental results reported today in Houston will be tested tomorrow in Beijing and Bombay. The tragedy of our times may well be that the sciences of society and man do not have a similar structure.

We mentioned above that the history of the science and art of cartography demonstrated important aspects of Issar's thesis — the movement along the information dimension through which the mytho-poetic and theological were displaced by hard science. The exploration of the biosphere had followed a similar course. Benjamin Franklin's kite experiment that demonstrated the electrical nature of lightning relegated the great god Thor and other deities of wind and storm to the pages of children's books of mythology.

It is a truism to say that every branch of science, indeed every branch of scholarship, has contributed to our current understanding of the biosphere and the current threat to its stability. The concept of the biosphere as a focus of scientific investigation is a product of the twentieth century and owes much to the work of the Russian geochemist, Vladimir Vernadsky. By his time the explorers had completed the investigation of the earth's surface. As early as the 1680s one of the first thematic maps had been compiled through the efforts of Edmund Haley (of comet fame). He had captained probably the first purely scientific voyage to map the variations of compass readings. Shortly thereafter there were entered data concerning prevailing winds and ocean currents. The momentous voyage of H.M.S. Beagle carrying Charles Darwin would, within a generation, remake the intellectual vision of homo sapiens. As more and more technology became available, balloons would carry meteorological instruments into the stratosphere. In the 1920s (as the age of radio began) the ionosphere will be discovered. The jet stream will be discovered by Japanese and American bomber pilots flying the Pacific between 1942 and 1944. Sputnik was launched in 1957, and it is important to note that this was a project intended to be part of the International Geophysical Year. The internationalization of the study of the biosphere was now in place, and satellites will discover the Van Allen radiation belt. And these splendid instruments will permit the continual monitoring of the biosphere.

It was Vernadsky who in the 1920s uttered a prophetic warning — human industrial activity, he said, has assumed the proportions of a geological force. A current issue of the newsletter, *The Washington Spectator* (January 1993), provides us with the raw data of this warning, stating that the world has exploited more of its mineral resources in the last twenty years than in all preceding history, and that in the United States alone mineral consumption from 1948 to 1976 exceeded that of all humanity up to 1940. We should note that the aforementioned statistics fulfill Vernadsky's prophecy that man will become a dangerous geological force.

Ever since his appearance as a developed species, Homo sapiens has been reshaping that part of the planetary landscape within his reach. And from earliest times the results have often been catastrophic. From the Indus valley to Morocco, Homo sapiens, the agriculturist, the builder of ships and cities, has created deserts. That this process continues as we move toward the twenty-first century should surprise no one. An ecological conscience for all of mankind is the present utopian hope. The inventory of potential calamities is well known: ozone depletion, global warming, desertification, exhaustion of fish stocks of the ocean, destruction of forests, soil erosion on every continent, pollution on an unimaginable scale, and a population explosion which magnifies all of the other processes of planetary deterioration. Malthus warned of this decades ago. However, well into the twentieth century, commissars and cardinals, and other holy men ignored the human tragedies that could not be concealed. The former thought that social revolution could bring about conditions that could accommodate an ever-growing population. They were indifferent or ignorant of the fact that any given area of the earth, however fertile, had a limited carrying capacity. The holy men, drawing on bad biology and dubious theology, opposed any effort to spread contraceptive methods of population control. They seemed oblivious to the fact that by restricting sexual intercourse to the act of breeding, they reduce human beings to the status of the beasts of the field. The mathematical equations that demographers use to project population growth and the doubling time for any given population are rather simple. They can be taught in high schools, and one assumes also in seminaries, corporate board rooms, and taught to the general public.

While preparing these pages, I was reminded of a startling fact I came across some twenty years ago: There is in England a species of raven which, when climate and other factors decrease the available food supply, prevent juvenile ravens from nesting.

Will Homo sapiens exhibit the same intelligence? Perhaps we should let Edgar Allen Poe's melancholy bird answer for us — 'Nevermore' *Jamais plus, nunca jamas, niemals mehr* — the reader should fill in the blank with his own language.

One should add that in recent years an understanding of the environmental crisis has spread widely around the world. International conferences have led to steps to reduce the use of ozone destroying chemicals. There is a growing awareness that the burning of fossil fuels must be curtailed. Green parties have emerged in scores of nations and some have achieved sufficient power to influence environmental legislation. The United States has recently elected a Vice President who is a knowledgeable and committed environmentalist.

With the lifting of the fifty year menace of thermonuclear war, optimists now see the possibility that the United Nations might coordinate all ongoing efforts to understand and preserve the biosphere. It would, however, be blind folly to believe that, without a fundamental shift in popular values, very much can be accomplished through any kind of purely political arrangement. At the heart of the crisis is the global structure of industrialism whose owners and managers have convinced themselves that only through the continual expansion of production can the underdeveloped world be brought to the level of the material well being of the so-called First World. If what we have listed above is correct, then the cry of 'jobs and development' is not a viable policy statement. Our descendants, if we are lucky, might look back on this proscription as nothing better than skin-clad Neanderthals dancing around a wood fire, supplicating their gods for deliverance.

When scholars have thought anew, presenting their theories and conjectures, their task is done. To act anew is the burden of the species.

Robert G. Colodny
Professor Emeritus
University of Pittsburgh
April 9, 1993

8 Postscript and epilogue

While I was preparing this book according to my publisher's instructions, I got a phone call from my friend Yigeal Granot from the Ben-Gurion College. He sounded rather excited. He told me he had some interesting news for me. He had just read an article in the latest Issue of *Scientific American.* In that essay a young philosopher at Washington University asserted that information is a dimension like space and time! When I got my copy of this journal, I indeed found there a very interesting article by John Horgan (1994), in which he summarized the discussions held during a meeting at the University of Arizona in Tucson. The subject of the meeting was 'Toward a Scientific Basis of Consciousness.'

One of the main issues discussed by the scientists who gathered at this meeting was whether consciousness can be explained by the experimental sciences, especially neurobiology, or does it belong to a mysterious domain which will elude experimental probing. One of the scientists, Dr David, J. Chalmers from Washington University, labeled by the writer in *Scientific American* as a 'mysterian', claimed that no physical theory, whether based on quantum mechanisms or neural ones can explain consciousness. Yet, he maintained that philosophers can and must construct a higher level theory to bridge that 'explanatory gap' between the physical and the subjective realms. In order to do this Chalmers asserts: that just as physics assumes the existence of properties in nature such as space, time, energy, charge, and mass, so must the theory of consciousness point to the existence of a new fundamental property which is information (Horgan, 1994, p. 78).

The reader may rightly assume that I agree with Dr Chalmers' suggestion that we consider information as a dimension equivalent to space and time. Yet I must argue against the use of the adjective 'mysterious' which was adapted and which still clings to his mode of explanation. I maintain that once this direction of thought is adapted, consciousness will not be a mystery and can be investigated as an ordinary scientific problem. By this I mean the formulation of hypotheses which can be tested through its predictions. To clarify my point of view, I suggest that we imagine ourselves to be present at an interdisciplinary, intertemporal meeting of physicists, astronomers, and philosophers discussing the question as to whether or not physics will be able to explain gravity. Newton would have mentioned that there is no mystery in it, since the ether is a physical material which exists and which transfers force according to his mechanical laws, and thus gravity is just a physical mechanical force. Michaelson and Morley would come up and claim that they did not detect any difference in the velocity of two beams of light, one sent in the direction of the rotation of the earth, and the other in the opposite direction. Their conclusion from their experiment is that no such physical substance as ether exists. Another scientist by the name of Maxwell would intervene and say, in speaking of light, which is an electromagnetic wave, he has developed a theory which enables him to explain the force between magnets and the production of an electric current when a wire rotates between the magnets. He calls this an electromagnetic field. He might then suggest that the participants examine the conceptual direction of the field and perhaps in that manner unveil the mystery of gravity. Most physicists, still awed by Newton's authority, will claim that although this new concept of a field of force explains magnetism and electricity, it still leaves the explanation of gravity, without the ether, a mystery, as a force must have some carrier in order to act on distant bodies. Einstein would probably try to impress upon the participants of this meeting that they should attempt to break through a psychological barrier and consider gravity as a field of force existing in a space-time four dimensional manifold. He will then describe gravity as a manifestation of the geometry of this manifold. He might even suggest some experiment that would verify this extraordinary new vision.

If one examines these arguments which actually took place, though not in my imaginary space-time location, one will find that a veil of mystery has always surrounded physical phenomena when the human observers insist on clinging to old, outmoded ways of thought. There was a time in the early 19th century when the behavior of a compass needle could not be explained. The eternal law-like motion of the celestial bodies found no physical explanation. But we must be careful to note that each discovery, filling in a gap in our knowledge, leads the probing mind to new areas of ignorance, and thus comes the undiminished impulse for further probing at the frontiers of existing science. The question remains as to whether or not mankind will eventually eliminate all mysteries and arrive finally at a 'theory of everything'.

An examination of this problem by the astronomer John D. Barrow, in his book *Theories of Everything* (1992), concludes as follows:

> There is no formula that can deliver all truth, all harmony, all simplicity. No theory of everything can ever provide total insight. For to see through everything, would be to see nothing at all. (P. 210)

This conclusion is in agreement with the conceptual model elaborated in my book. It asserts that human progress along the space-time-information dimension takes place against the pull of entropy. Here is to be found the arrow of evolution from primeval chaos to infinite intelligence. This process has no terminal point because our universe itself expands always creatively, and since its dimensions are intrinsic to its architecture, it determines the continuity of the expansion of the horizons of understanding by intelligent beings. This ever-receding goal of the intellect should not lead to scientific agnosticism or to despair. The achievements of science up to our time guarantee that, as long as man does not lose hope and turns his mind and effort against discernible ignorance, knowledge will expand. If I had the power to do so, I would outlaw the term 'mystery' from the vocabulary of scientists and replace it by the phrase 'Hitherto unexplained observations.' This not as a mere semantic game. It helps direct human intelligence towards a solution of the unexplained, and tends to undermine adherence to prejudices. (Some of the above observations were hinted at in the very beginning of modern science by Sir Francis Bacon. (*))

In a return to the problem of consciousness, I reiterate that this issue has been wrapped in prejudice. We should note that classical neurobiology, based only on space-time physics and chemistry, will not be sufficient to bring us to a final solution. This does not mean that efforts in this field are meaningless. They shed light on the relation between sense data and the flow of neuronal activity. Yet from this point on, I maintain that clarification can come about only by utilization of the dimension of information. But it should be noted that in my total overview of this ancient problem, it is necessary to incorporate the entropy-order field within which conscious thought and action are embedded. When one inquires as to which of the scientific disciplines may shed light here the answer is:

quantum physics. The reader may find the reason for this in Chapter 4 of this book.

An effort to explain consciousness by employing quantum mechanics was undertaken by Dana Zohar and Ian Marshall (Zohar, 1991, Marshall, 1992, Zohar and Marshall, 1993). I came upon these works after I had completed this book, a fact which I regret, but I also draw satisfaction from this intersection of thoughts by noting that my primary idea, that consciousness should be measured along the dimension of information, is consistent with a quantum physics model. Furthermore, after a careful study of their work, I have the conviction that my conceptual model can readily be merged with theirs, and we would thus have a radically new view of the mind-body problem which would be beautiful to contemplate.

Before summarizing their model, I will elaborate a bit more on consciousness in its relation to intelligence. As the reader may have noted already, I put the emphasis on intelligence rather than on consciousness. The reason for this is the emphasis I put on evolution (in the most general sense of this term). In order to understand the principles of evolution, one needs a careful account of the response of living organisms to stimuli which flow continuously from the environment. It is my conclusion that the difference between consciousness and intelligence is in operational aspects. While the first quality is the more passive aspect of the interaction between an organism and its environment, the second quality describes the active one which interfaces with behavior. In this respect, I remind the reader of the definition of intelligence quoted in Chapter 1, which asserted that the difference between instinct and intelligence is the ability to develop a new mode of reaction when an entirely novel situation is encountered (Bitterman, 1976). Thus while consciousness is a basic condition for all forms of life, its manifestation may be in instinctive as well as intelligent reaction. Intelligence is a relative parameter. The response of bacteria and a human being to any change in the environment will be a manifestation of their consciousness (awareness), while the difference between the quality of their responses will be a tentative measure of their intelligence. In the terminology of the space-time-information model, consciousness is defined as the active state of any natural system while it reacts along the dimension of information. (The reader is warned against using this definition as a definition of life, because this would be falling into a tautology. Recall that information was defined as that which is measured by the brain, or a computer, created by a conscious brain.)

The reason that Zohar and Marshall concluded that consciousness is something which has to be treated in the domain of quantum mechanics was, in the first place, a consequence of their conclusion that the unity of consciousness is a reflection of the unified material structure of the brain. (The whole dominates and integrates the parts). Hence classical physics, especially Newtonian mechanics which views matter as composed of individual atoms interacting by force, by depriving any substrate of its unity, cannot treat the problem of consciousness. Quantum mechanics, on the other hand, treats a system composed of many particles of the same type as one unified system in which each particle is indistinguishable from the other. A unified physical system which fulfills this requirement of unity is that found in the Bose-Einstein Condensate. In this system the many components respond as a unified whole. The changes that it undergoes are those of phase differences, such as the order of the system. This approach touches also on the problem of the observer's influence on the results of quantum experiment. This subtle problem is intrinsic in quantum mechanics. (It is discussed briefly in Chapter 4.) It is also referred to in numerous writings about Schrödinger's (wretched) Cat. This is a consequence of one interpretation of the collapse of the wave function. Basically, in quantum mechanics one deals with probabilities rather than with deterministic results. According to the orthodox Copenhagen Theory (Einstein dissenting), this is not a result of the limitations of the measurement process, but reflects an absolute reality. According to the model of Zohar and Marshall, in a Bose-Einstein Condensate the collapse of the wave function is into a phase difference rather than a space difference. This means that the collapse which has to happen somehow, happens spontaneously and produces those kinds of states in the brain which are responsible for consciousness (Marshall, 1992, p. 107).

The Bose-Einstein Condensate in the terminology of my model will be an entropy-order field in which changes are measured along time-information coordinates, while space is a constant. Thus its response to any excitation will be an indivisible whole expressed in a change of the level of its order. The excitation itself, which can be described as a collapsed event, is not more and not less than a transformation of a certain event measured along space-time coordinates (when information is constant), into an event measured along time-information coordinates (space-constant). Such a collapse will re-occur, in the opposite direction, when the mental picture will be transformed into a specific pattern as a reaction of the living cell or organism. The collapse of the wave function, once the dimension of information is considered, can also be applied to the problem of the cosmic constants which invited the formulation of the much debated anthropic principle. This problem is discussed in Chapter 4, but there without reference to the collapse of the wave function. It was suggested there to modify the solution suggested by Carter (1974) and Wheeler (1976), which speaks of a future intelligent observer implicit in the Big Bang as a precondition guaranteeing the evolution of life. The conceptual model in this book suggests that the Big Bang, or any other act of creation, involved — in addition to the coming into existence of the dimensions of space-time and the four fields of force (gravity, electro-magnetic and the weak and strong forces) — the dimension of information and the field of entropy-order. These were the conditions when the physical environment was appropriate for the emergence of a system within which evolved an intelligent observer. Now using the conceptual model, which involved the language describing the collapse of the wave function, one can say that out of the infinite probabilities implicit in the states of wave functions which followed the events of creation, the collapse was into the unique state which ensured the evolution of consciousness and ultimately an intelligent observer.

The arrow of time intrinsic in the field of entropy-order tells us also something about the two possible directions which might have taken place once the pre-biotic wave collapsed. One direction is backwards into disorder, namely death, the other into a more ordered system, namely a higher level of conscious self-multiplying substance. This could have happened an endless number of times during billions of years when numberless dead ends may have been reached and passed into oblivion. Yet once the initial system survived to form an evolved state, a momentum was gained and evolution took off towards a more intelligent form of life.

This brings us back to the question of chance versus necessity discussed in Chapter 5. The constraints of the field of entropy-order in the framework of a space-time-information dimension system decides two fundamental properties of all forms of life. The first one has to do with the impulse to survive inherent in every living organism, and the second fundamental property, just mentioned above, which is the basic argument of my book, namely the progressive movement of evolution up the scale of intelligence.

Regarding the first fundamental property, no scientist today argues with the main conclusion of Darwin that the origin of species is the result of the survival of the organism with the most adaptive mutations. This refers to a selection process enforced by the constraints of the environment. This theory takes for granted that there exists an inbred mechanism in all forms of life which permits them to display a variety of mutations. The question now is whether this mechanism is due to chance and thus is not directed toward survival, or on the contrary, is it a purposeful mechanism produced to guarantee survival? Most biologists will shun this question, accusing anyone who raises it of attempting to impose an anthropomorphic mode of thought (one should not import purposefulness into a purposeless nature). There is no reason why one should not question even the human will to survive. One might even suggest that this impulse is carried by our DNA from remote prehuman times. What we know of the will for survival of the higher animals permits the raising of this question: why does the mechanism of mutation, which enabled both survival and evolution, come into existence in the first place if there was no purpose in survival? The physicists ask, as a matter of fact, a similar question when they investigate the reasons which keeps physical bodies together or which permit them to evolve, as in the building of crystals. Since these objects are inanimate they do not ask the question about the will of atoms, molecules, or crystals to survive, but instead seek for a general physical law or force which controls the process. Today physics has elucidated the nature of the four fields of force which operate in the inanimate world, though when it comes to the bioworld, the biologists, in the main, are more catholic than the Pope; and since they are afraid to be labeled as being nonobjective in their scientific attitudes, they avoid any questions which evoke teleonomy. Let us brave this taboo and look for a force outside the organism which can ground survival processes. I think we will find it in the field of entropy-order. Progress in this field along the dimensions of space-time produce the many forms of life, while movement along the dimension of information controls the evolution of the bioworld towards more intelligent forms. This model breaks another taboo, that of Lamarckism. It suggests that certain acquired properties become heritable. It goes beyond that to suggest that the sequence of mutations which are ubiquitous in the bioworld are biased towards survival. To be more explicit the new theory asserts that a certain form of life, opposing extinction, will develop those mutations which, within a change in environment, will enable it to survive. As I have said, this may be a form of neo-Lamarckism — thus a heresy as viewed from Darwinism and neo-Darwinism. To avoid the equivalent of being burnt at the stake, one must provide a natural event or successful experiment. In the well-known case of the giraffe with a extendible neck, for instance, it would have been interesting to put all the giraffes in all the zoos in the world with their food, above the average height of a giraffe, and then wait to see whether or not the giraffes in the zoos became taller. This of course would take too long. Here we will have to be content with experiments carried out on bacteria, for instance, the experiment which was brought to my attention by Marshall (1992) and performed by Hall (1991). This experiment involved two mutations in the genes of bacteria which caused them to stop synthesizing tryptophane, which is an essential life ingredient. Thus, on nutrient plates containing a very small amount of this ingredient, the bacteria started to die off. But after about three weeks it was found that both mutations had been corrected to a form which could synthesize tryptophane. The process of the correction most probably followed the Darwinian algorithm of the survival of those bacteria which produced mutations which corrected the previous mutations, and thus permitted the synthesis by them of tryptophane. This would not have been the model suggested in this book, unless this correction of the mutated genes had not been a hundred million times faster than any purely random process model. This is one of the many experiments which were reported recently in the scientific literature (Marshall, 1992).

In conclusion one may say that a trend of necessity can be observed in the pre-biotic cosmos as well as in the bioworld. In the first the necessity is manifested by the anthropic principle, while in the second it can be seen in the neo-Lamarckian phenomena just discussed. This necessity, or even a marked trend from a low to a higher level of organization on space-time-information coordinates, cannot be explained if one looks for the cause in the organism itself. This would repeat the mistake that many philosophers committed when they looked for the reason for the apple to fall in the apple itself (Newton). One should look for the source of the impulse to survive, and thus form more evolved entity in that general field of entropy-order that is intrinsic in the cosmos.

This brings us to the question implicit in the first chapter of this book, namely: did the geologist find a creator and if so, how can he describe him or it? The answer is that indeed the creator was found, but behold, it is creation itself. It is the magnificent, colossal edifice called self, society, and nature, the laws of which one struggles to understand. It started according to what current physicists hypothesize in a singular event, most probably the Big Bang, following a state of total chaos of infinite entropy and infinite gravity. During the singular event at the beginning of creation, the dimensions of space-time-information, and the movement against the fields of entropy and gravity started. During this movement the other fields of forces came into being, each becoming effective when the cosmic environment was ready. The general field seems to be that of entropy, and a general trend of cosmic evolution is from a state of total chaos towards infinite organized information along the dimensions of maximum space-time. This can also be illustrated as an endless movement of unfolding, revealing higher levels or ordered space-time-information. Thus appear more and more intelligent organized entities, the ultimate goal being infinite intelligence in infinite space-time. In this movement are encompassed the laws of physics, biology, psychology, behavior, and sociology. This movement supports the tendency of the atom, molecule, organism, and society to survive. It is the reason for the instinct of the bee to sacrifice its life to protect the queen of the hive, the soldier to risk his existence for his country, the feelings of love between cat and kitten, mother and child, man and woman, feelings of friendship between individuals and communities, laws of justice and righteousness. This striving for peaceful coexistence as well as the drive towards competition and success. This colossal, magnificent perpetual movement, as for all movements in a field of force which are influenced by opposing poles — takes the form of waves. It moves forward, but on an oscillating curve, up and down. We find it manifested by the flourishing and expansion of species over land, the seas, and the air. We find it also in their degeneration and even extinction. It is displayed in the prosperity of empires and their collapse, the flourishing of religions, ideologies, and philosophies, and the eventual abandonment of each. Thus we can conclude that each theory, religion, and ideology, once formulated, bears within it the seed of its degeneration as time passes. Yet the drive of evolution on ordered space-time-information is eternal; the decay of a once-thriving system reveals a sprout of a newer, younger, and more advanced system.

9 Appendix: From the lower part of Tiamat to the Law of D'Arcy

> And God made the firmament, and divided the waters which were under the firmament from the waters which were above the firmament: and it was so. And God called the firmament Heaven.
>
> Genesis 1:6-7

The subject discussed in this appendix is an illustration of the hypothesis that the evolution of science is progress in the opposite direction to the pole of entropy in the framework of a space-time-information coordinate system. Thus, the process of the evolution of a scientific theory involves observations, i.e. space-time events, interconnected by logical reasoning, i.e. organized along the dimension of information, constructed in the field of entropy-order. The more advanced the theory, the higher its position in this field. The case serving as an illustration is the evolution of the theory of ground water.

As water is a prime factor in man's life he paid it special attention and tried from the very beginning of his history to formulate conceptual models to explain the various phenomena he observed. While mankind's culture was still in its infancy, and as most of the laws of nature were hidden behind a heavy curtain of ignorance, man invented divine powers and gave them full responsibility for what happens around him, and to him personally. Thus, it can be claimed that the first conceptual models were the religious. These were characterized by man's habit to regard himself as the center of the universe and his conviction that nature was created for his purpose. As a consequence he found a correlation between the events he observed in nature and his own impulses, reactions and actions. He anthropomorphized the processes he observed in nature. The evolution of science was connected with mankind's gradual escape from this anthropocentric attitude. Yet at the stage of the childhood of humanity these were the basic approaches.

One of the first phenomena man tried to explain was that of water. The most ancient conceptual models which have survived are those written in Sumer in Mesopotamia about 4,500 years ago (Kramer, 1954). They tell the story of a universe composed only of water, namely a primeval sea which engendered a cosmic mountain consisting of heaven and earth united.

As Sumer was located in the lowlands of Mesopotamia near the outlet of the Tigris and Euphrates to the Persian Gulf, it had the same conditions as that of The Netherlands, in modern times. These conditions are characterized by the subsurface being saturated by saline sea water overlain by a thin layer of fresh water, supplied by precipitation as well as the floods of the big rivers traversing the country on their way to the sea. When the water of the river is low, due to a dry year, the thickness and level of the fresh water layer recedes and the saline sea water encroaches into the river inlets and the subsurface. At present the decrease of the flow of rivers, as a function of the quantity of precipitation on the catchment areas, can be calculated, and then the rate of recession of the fresh water body and accordingly the penetration of the sea water can be forecasted. The Sumerians did not connect the lowering of the water in their rivers with the encroachment of the sea into the rivers and subsurface. In their conceptual model the interconnection between the observations was in the opposite direction. They explained to themselves the recession of the water of the river as a result of the fact that Kur the great god of the primeval waters, symbolizing the saline water of the sea as well as the subsurface water, got furious at Niuntra the god of the South Wind. It is narrated in a Sumerian myth how Kur rises in anger and then the rivers do not rise, famine is severe, the water in the small rivers does not rise, the fields are not irrigated, and there are no crops only weeds. Niuntra solves the problem by building in the river dikes against the encroaching sea water. This engineering device, which the Dutch people are going to adopt about four millennia later, stops the flow of the fresh water into the sea and brings up its level to irrigate the fields, and recharges the body of fresh water underground, which pushes back the interface between the fresh and saline ground water. Thus, an hydrological calamity and a feat of clever engineering are reported in the form of a conceptual model, which involves the forces of nature expressed as anthropomorphic gods. This explanation was most logical to the hypothesizing mind of the ancients. It is evident that the king or the irrigation engineer who devised and ordered the construction of the dikes understood that the recession of the rivers and the upheaval of the sea are interconnected. Ancient man might not have understood that the low level of the Tigris and Euphrates are due to a spell of dry climate, namely less rains on the Zagros mountains and thus less floods. He was living at the outlet of the rivers which was at that time north of the present confluence of the Euphrates and Tigris to the Shat-el Arab. These lowlands are arid and all irrigation is dependent on these rivers. The encroachment of the sea might have been enhanced by a global rise in the sea level due to a climate change which caused the glaciers at the poles to melt. We would not expect this man who lived between the Zagros mountains and the Arabian desert to understand all this; what he sees and understands is the change in the balance between the water of the river and the water of the sea. He finds a way to ameliorate such a change. This however is not sufficient, he has to explain what happened and to suggest a theory. The closest conceptual model for this and his fellows' comprehension is a fight between two groups of people ruled by their kings. Each group has its protecting deity symbolizing a force of nature, which is crucial to the survival of its protectorates. Thus the model sought to explain what happened and what was done involved such a fight; and victory was gained in this case by a clever device rather than by physical strength. Something similar yet less personified happened about two hundred years ago when men observed electromagnetic phenomena. The closest conceptual model was that of hydrodynamics. Thus, we speak today of an electrical current, and flow of electricity.

Another 'hydrological' conceptual model to explain the relation between surface water and ground water is the story of creation told in the *Enuma Elish,* which is the book of genesis of the Babylonians. It starts with the following lines:

> When in the height heaven was not named,
> And the earth beneath did not yet bear a name,
> And the primeval Apsu who begat them,
> And chaos Tiamat the mother of them both,
> Their waters were mingled together,
> And no field was formed, no marsh was to be seen;
> When the gods none had been called into being,
> And none bore a name, and no destinies were ordained.
>
> (King, 1951)

In this story Tiamat is the Mother Goddess representing also the primeval abyss of water, while her spouse Apsu is in charge on the sweet water ocean. They plan to kill all the other gods because they disturb their sleep. Apsu is killed in the first encounter, and when Tiamat wants to avenge the killing of her spouse, Murduch the son of the god Ea fights against her and her followers, and kills her.

> Then the lord rested, gazing upon her dead body,
> While he divided the flesh of the trunk,
> and devised a cunning plan.
> He split her up like a flat fish into two halves;
> One half of her he established as a covering for heaven.
> He fixed a bolt he stationed a watchman,
> And bade them not to let her waters come forth.
>
> (King, 1951)

Thus the ancient Babylonians had a conceptual model to explain the fact that water falls from heaven, and water is found in the subsurface. As one can see, while Murduch inserted valves with a watchmen to keep the upper water from flowing out, no valves were needed in the lower part for the water of the deep. The force of gravity was taken for granted in this ancient hydrological conceptual model.

A rather similar hydrological theory, or even paradigm, is found in the Bible. In the first place the story of creation in the book of Genesis takes it for granted that the water is a primeval entity already existing before the seven days of genesis. (The word 'Tehom' in the Hebrew version, which was translated into 'the face of the deep' on which the 'spirit of God was moving' has undoubtedly its roots in the ancient Babylonian Goddess 'Tiamat' representing the primeval abyss). In the second place the water of skies is divided from the water of the deep by a firmament. The main difference between the Babylonian conceptual model of Murdoch dividing Tiamat and the Jewish one, which involves a God ordering the installment of the firmament, is the means by which the division of the waters between that of skies and the deep is accomplished. While the Babylonians believed that the gods fight and kill each other like human beings, the Jews maintained that the one God is above such human frivolities.

The hydrological paradigm, of the water of the heavens locked up, and the water of the great deep (*Tehom raba,* in Hebrew), forming an underground ocean, is apparent also in the story of the deluge, as one can see from the biblical story of the deluge.

... the same day were all the fountains of the great deep broken up, and the windows of heaven were opened. (Genesis 7:11)

The most ancient narration of the story of the deluge is apparently the Sumerian one. It was adopted by the Babylonians and Assyrians, and is repeated in the Bible. In the story of the deluge too, the reason for it is given according to the world view of the people narrating it. In the mythologies of the people of Mesopotamia, the deluge comes upon the land because the gods were fighting, while in the Jewish biblical version the reason is the punishment by God for the corruption of the people.

The conceptual model suggested by the present author is that indeed a flood affected the Mesopotamian plain at the dawn of history, the cause for it being a global climate change causing the glaciers to expand and rain storms to sweep over the Mediterranean, reaching the Levant. This caused floods over the lowlands. One of the reasons for bringing up this suggestion, on top of the paleo-climatic evidence is the fact that in all the ancient narrations, although written in a land of rivers, the reason for the floods are rains and flow of fountains, and not floods coming from the rivers. This shows that the deluge was an anomaly for the people living in a region in which floods are normal. The anomaly was that of rains and high water table, which caused springs to emerge everywhere. There is no better conceptual model than a 'climate change', to explain such a change, leaving an impression on the people of Mesopotamia to be told to their descendants for many generations to come. (Issar, 1990)

The ancient Greeks were also concerned about the origin of springs. Greece is a Mediterranean country where most rains fall in winter. Summers are long, hot and mostly dry. Thus in this season the water supply depends on the flow of the springs issuing in many cases from limestone caverns. The Greek mythology regarded the springs as the place of the residence of Pan, one of their gods who enjoyed playing the flute made of reeds growing everywhere water was flowing.

In the 6th and 5th century B.C. in Greece there was an active school of scientists-philosophers who combined observation and logic to explain the phenomena of nature. They are called 'The Pre-Socratics'. They are also referred to as the Ionian Nature Philosophers. They were involved in a movement of thought which was divided between philosophy of mind and theories about natural processes. Although they were influenced by ideas derived from the older civilizations of the Near East, they were not overwhelmed by them (Hussey, 1972). It can be claimed that this school was the first attempt by man to use non-religious conceptual models and theories in order to explain nature.

Thales asserted that water was the primordial substance, i.e. all things could be created of it. In his recent book, *Dreams of a Final Theory*, the Nobel Laurette, Steven Weinberg (Physics and Cosmology) asserts that Thales should be considered the father of that endless search for the theory that explains everything (Weinberg, 1994) One of its most astonishing and often cited achievements was that of Leucippus and Democritus of Abdera, who claimed that an indivisible entity, namely the atom is the building block of all observable materials.

The atomistic tradition was embedded in the work of Epicurus. His follower, Lucretius, carried these ideas into the Roman world. In his great nature poem, *De Rerum Natura*, the implicit atheism of his doctrine antagonized the Roman patricians. In one of his letters Cicero wrote something to the effect that Lucretius had produced a work of art, but it could not be circulated in Rome, because if the mob lost its fear of the gods, how could they be controlled? The Renaissance recovered Lucretius' poem and in the 17th century the French priest, Pierre Gassendi, who was a friend of Galileo and Keppler, wrote an essay purging atomism of any connection with atheism. Newton made the best of both worlds by asserting that in the beginning God created the atoms in such number and form as to fulfill his eternal purposes. (*)

An advanced theory, considering the time of its formulation, for explaining the phenomena of springs was suggested by the pre-Socratic philosopher Anaxagoras of Clazomnea (who lived from 500 to 428 B.C.). We do not have his writings, but fortunately Aristotle, who lived about a hundred years later, refutes him after citing him first in his book *Meteorologica* (his and Aristotle's hydrology are discussed by Adams, 1938). Anaxagoras maintained that all ground water is due to the rains which are raised by the sun (evaporation) to fall on the earth and gather below it in great reservoirs. Due to this the rivers which are fed from the springs are fuller in winter when the subterranean reservoirs are full, and diminish in summer when these reservoirs empty. Some of them dry up when their vessels empty before the fresh rains come. He also maintained that no water is generated during its flow through the hydrological cycle. This is the first pronouncement of the principle of conservation of matter.

Anaxagoras also asserted that the sun was composed of flaming rock and was probably as large as the Peleponnesus. For this leap of intuition Anaxagoras was accused of impiety which would have had lethal consequences but for the intervention of the Athenian leader, Pericles. (*)

As already mentioned, Aristotle did not agree with Anaxagoras' hydrological theory, although his teacher Plato did adopt it. The reason for Aristotle's disagreement was his claim that the volume of water is much greater than the volume of the earth, in which it was assumed to be stored. He thus suggested another conceptual model which maintained that water is formed continuously in the earth from air which was considered to be a sort of aqueous vapor. It seems also that he believed that juvenile water is added from the depths. As the generators for transforming air into water he suggested the high mountains which cool the vapors that rise from the lowlands and condense it into water.

In this conceptual model, Aristotle tried to explain as many as possible of his meteorological and hydrological observations in one logical, reasonable theory. In the first place, it seemed to him that quantitatively the volume of water flowing out as springs and rivers is more than the volume of the earth from which it comes. So he had to explain volume without storage for which continuous generation is needed.

In his conceptual model, Aristotle incorporated two paradigms which were fundamental to his world view. The first concerned the four elements from which the world was built, and which possessed properties. Fire possessed heat, earth coldness, water dampness and air dryness. The second paradigm was that by the combination of these elements the different materials were formed. He also believed that air and water are related and can thus be transformed each into other. This must have come from the observation that when heat and water are combined the latter turns into vapor. Another observation was the condensation of water on cold stones. To these, one had to add the observation that on high mountains the air is colder and there is snow. Other observations taken into account were that big springs issue at the feet of these high mountains, and that in the caves, which are abundant in the limestone mountains of which the main part of Greece is built, water trickles down from the fractures. The construction of the puzzle, for which the principle of the four elements and the formation of materials is the framework, resulted in the Aristotelian 'logical' theory of the formation of springs. The basic empirical flaw of this theory, on top of the erroneous 'theoretical' foundation of the 'basic elements'; was that its initial observation was erroneous, namely that the volume of the water is much greater than that of the earth. Thus, although Aristotle's theory was a beautiful ordered structure on the dimension of information, it did not correlate with the real world, and at the end had to be abandoned. Two thousand years had to pass, however, before Aristotle's theory was transferred to the wastebasket of scientific theories.

The Romans, who adopted the Hellenistic philosophical and scientific paradigms were practical people. Their engineers did not ask too many philosophical questions. They looked for perennial springs as a source of water, but were satisfied as long as the quantity ensured a safe and ongoing supply of water. They liked these springs to be on a higher altitude than their cities, thus they had enough pressure to have the water flow in the beautifully constructed aqueducts, and come out as fountains in the midst of their cities. They were thus more interested in developing the methods of measuring the rate of flow of the springs, and the right planning and construction of their aqueducts, than understanding the mysteries of ground water flow. When perennial springs were not available in the vicinity of cities in the more arid part of their empire, they knew how to excavate wells and reach ground water. This they learnt most probably from the local people, who knew since proto-historical periods, how to locate and use ground water (Issar, 1990).

Aristotelian views had been adopted by the Christian church and were taught in its schools to the monks and priests who formed the literate class. They were not accepted, however, indiscriminately. They had to conform with the Holy Scriptures, and a big part of the 'scientific' research during the Middle Ages, and also centuries later in many of the monasteries, was devoted to interpreting Aristotelian' views according to the Bible and the other convictions of the church. The writings of the Bible were for these monks a basic truth, like any other indubitable observation of nature. As a matter of fact Aristotelian writings and the Bible had more authority than any observation, and thus provided the factual data upon which the world view of man had to be based. From the Space-time-information model point of view, one can say that the 'scientific thinking' of the church was restricted to structures on the dimension of information, the source of which were the scriptures and Aristotle's writings.

One could even find complementary evidence in these two main sources of information. The hydrological paradigm of the ancients, echoed in Genesis, of the Firmament dividing between the upper and lower waters, was rather in conformity with Aristotelian views. He also divided the cosmos into spheres according to the elements.

The same conformity was found within the passage in Ecclesiastics (1, 7) which reads, 'All the rivers run into the sea, yet the sea is not full unto the place from which the rivers come thither they return again'. During the Middle Ages, to the explanation by Aristotle of the of water by condensation, was added that of water drawn into the earth from the sea by whirlpools flowing underground in submarine and subterrain galleries. These become purified underground and then flow out as springs, which supply the rivers, which flow to the sea and so on and so forth. This explanation was brought up by Kircher who was a Jesuit. In his book, *Mundus Subterraneans*, which was published in Amsterdam in 1678, he suggested that there are holes in the sea bottom which communicate with the caverns in the mountains and due to various processes the waters are made to flow upward and are able to fulfill what was stated in the Bible. Numerous other scholarly manipulations and tricks of the mind were performed by pious people in order to answer the controversies between the Holy Scriptures, Aristotle and the hydrological phenomena observed in nature. A description of these the reader will find in Chapter XII, called 'The Origin of Springs and Rivers' in Adams' book, mentioned above.

The unbiased understanding of what really happens in nature came at the time when man was able to free himself of the obligation to regard the ancient writings as truths, more to be trusted than what his eyes see. In other words only the breaking away from the dogmatic paradigms of the church enabled European man to believe in what he observed in nature and permitted him to interpret his observations according to his common sense.

Once this happened, new conceptual models followed each other. These were invented by non-conformists, who searched to new answers for questions, which were thought by the majority of their contemporaries to have been answered. Such non-conventional thinkers were Leonardo da Vinci (1452-1519), and Bernard Palissy (1514-1589). They hypothesized that the water issuing as springs is just part of rainwater percolating through the porous and fractured layers. Another forerunner of modern hydrological theory was Blaise Pascal (1623-1662), who formulated correctly the laws of fluid pressure(*).

The proof of these conceptual models came when a quantitative approach was applied. This was done first by Pierre Penault, who in his book '*De l'Origine des Fontaines*' which was published at Paris in the year 1674, presented a quantitative hydrological balance of the drainage basin of the river Seine. This balance showed that all the water that was drained out by this river amounted only to about one sixth of the total rainfall on its catchment basin. This was followed, a few years later, by another set of measurements and calculations by the physicist Mariotte who modified it to about one-eighth. Other quantitative investigations which followed during the 18th century established the theory of the hydrological cycle, which one finds in the contemporary textbooks.

After the conceptual model became a theory and was established qualitatively and quantitatively, came the process of precise calculations. The engineer Henry D'Arcy calculated the flow of water through a porous medium and thus formulated what one finds in most text books as Darcy's Law. It states that the volume of water flowing through a certain section of a porous rock, is equal to the permeability of the rock, multiplied by the gradient of the water table. Further developments of this law for its application for various conditions was achieved by hydrologists during the, 19th and 20th centuries.

The invention and introduction of computers, enabled the processing of vast quantities of data, and the testing of various computerized flow models. These calculations could be accomplished in a matter of days and even hours, operations which once needed months and even years. Many hydrologists were at first euphoric with the new vistas opened up before them by computers. Some started to fantasize that in the future, only very few field investigations, aimed to supply some basic data would be needed. All the rest of the work would be done by the computer, which would manipulate the basic data, and will find the best adjustment between these observations and monitored control points. This approach reminds one of the belief of the people of Greece at the dawn of the classical era of philosophy, that logical reasoning based on just a few observations is sufficient to reveal the mysteries of nature. It took a rather short time to change the attitude of the computer models' partisans and to convince them that there is no electronic substitute for the hydrogeologist who investigates the natural environment, and in addition to data collection, suggests a few alternative conceptual models, to be tested by trial and error on the computer. The indispensability of the human mind and its capacity for innovation, is especially manifest in new terrain, or situations, when new conceptual models have to be invented. Problems, which involve the utilization of ground water, are investigated today by teams which include geologists who construct the conceptual models on the basis of observations taken in the field; chemists who investigate the isotopic and chemical composition of the water; physicists and mathematicians who construct the mathematical-physical computerized models; and engineers and economists who investigate the optimal policies for the utilization and management of the resource.

Yet, with all the knowledge which man acquired in the understanding of the laws of nature, and albeit all the wonderful observation, analysis and computing tools which he possesses, he was foolish enough, in many cases to cause society heavy damage, by polluting the environment. In many cases this damage is not reversible. Here we come to the other aspect of the evolution of the understanding of the works of nature, and the formulation of new scientific theories, brought up in connection with the difficulties expected in accepting information as a dimension. It was stated that man's understanding of nature progressed simultaneously with man's de-anthropocentralism, namely his gradual self shifting himself from the center of nature. As also discussed in this chapter, in the early stages of his efforts in explaining natural phenomena, man, consciously and subconsciously, imagined himself and the gods, (which he created in his own image) as situated at the center of the universe. All processes of nature were just a reflection of his fears, needs and deeds. Progressively, the laws suggested by man became more impersonal and more in conformity with nature. One can say that the progress of science was parallel with the expansion of the horizons of man's conceptual models, and their inter-dependence. Thus the more holistic his world view became, the better he understood the working of particular processes. The explanation offered in this book is that this shift from the man centered universe was a result of man's progress on the dimension of information, upwards and against the pull of entropy. Thus he became more intellectually mature, and this enabled him to see things as they are and not as he would like them to be. This also enabled him to form more holistic conceptual models.

Yet, mans' understanding did not always concur with his actions, especially when it involved the need to satisfy immediate needs. A survey of the many environmental mishaps connected with water resources development projects will show that the failures are a function of man's inability to approach the problem in an holistic way. For example, salination of soil processes which are due to over-irrigation, are in most cases because of the lack of taking into consideration the aspects of the movement of the water in the subsurface. This neglect, will also become a factor in pollution of soils and surface and ground water, as well as the neglect of existing knowledge of the chemical nature of the hazardous wastes.

Thus when it comes to an adequate approach to the environment, the paramount directive should be the holistic approach. In the field of water resources development it spells the need for understanding the entire regional hydrological cycle, starting from precipitation, which provides the resource, down to its surface and subsurface outlets. Man's intervention should thus take into consideration the whole system. Thus when he plans a water supply to a certain city, he should take into consideration not only the problem of supply, but also the problem of disposal, which will include the treatment of the changes in the chemical composition of the water due to its passing through its consumers. Fortunately, in many countries this comprehensive attitude is becoming routine in the requirements of bidders for regional water development projects. This gives hope that man's progress on the dimension of information, towards a more comprehensive, holistic world view, will manifest itself also in his attitude to the natural environment.

Bibliography

Adams, D.F. (1938), *The Birth and Development of the Geological Sciences*, Dover Publications, New York.

Aristotle (1943), *Politics*, Jowett, B. (trans.), Random House Modern Library, New York.

Barrow, J.D. (1992), *Theories of Everything, The Quest for Ultimate Explanation*, Vintage Edition, London

Bendall, D.S. (ed.), (1983), *Evolution from Molecules to Men*, Cambridge University Press.

Bergson, H. (1974), L'Évolution Créatrice, La Presse Universitaires de France, Paris. (Trans. into Hebrew by Ur, J.), The Magnes Press, The Hebrew University, Jerusalem.

Bitterman, A. (1965), The Evolution of Intelligence, *Scientific American*, January, pp. 92–94.

Brain, L. (1968), In Smythies, J.R. (ed.), *Brain and Mind*, Routledge and Kegan Paul, London.

Bunn, C. (1964), *Crystals, Their Role in Nature and in Science*, Academic Press Inc. New York.

Capra, F. (1975), *The Tao of Physics*, Wildwood House, London.

Carter, B. (1974), 'Large Number Coincidences and the Anthropic Principle in Cosmology', in Longair, M.S. (ed.), *Confrontations of Cosmological Theories with Observational Data*, Reidel, Dordrecht, pp. 291–298.

Clark, G. (1977), *World Prehistory in New Perspective*, Cambridge University Press, Cambridge.

Clark Howell, F. (1970), *Early Man*, Life-Nature Library, Time-Life International, Netherlands.

Commins, S. and Linscott, R.N. (eds.) (1954), *The World's Great Thinkers, Man and the Universe, The Philosophers of Science*, Modern Pocket Library, New York.

Darwin, C. (1959), *Evolution and Natural Selection*, An Anthology of the Writings of Charles Darwin, by B.J. Loewenberg (ed.), Beacon Press, Boston.

Davies, P.C.W. (1988), *The Cosmic Blueprint, New Discoveries in Nature's Creative Ability to Order the Universe*, Simon and Schuster, New York

Davies, P.C.W. and Brown, J.R. (1986), *The Ghost in the Atom*, Cambridge University Press, Cambridge.

Dawkins, G. (1986),*The Blind Watchmaker*, Longman Scientific and Technical Publications.

Dawkins, G.(1978), *The Selfish Gene*, Granada Publishing Ltd., London.

De Chardin, P.T. (1965), *The Phenomenon of Man*, Fontana Paperbacks, Great Britain.

Denbigh, K.G. (1989), 'Note on Entropy, Disorder and Disorganization', *British Journal of the Philosophy of Science.*, Vol. 40, pp. 323–332.

Dobzhansky, T. (1962), *Mankind Evolving, The Evolution of the Human Species*, Yale University Press, New Haven and London.

Eaton, R. M. (ed.) (1955), *Descartes Selections*, Charles Scribners Sons, New York.

Eddington, A. (1959), *Space, Time and Gravitation*, Harper & Brothers Publishers, New York.

Einstein, A. (1949), *The World As I See It*, Harris, A. (trans.), The Wisdom Library, A Division of Philosophical Library, New York.

Einstein, A. (1962), 'Relativity', in *Relativity and the Problem of Space*, University Paperbacks, Methuen Co., Ltd., London, Appendix V.

Eldredge, N. (1989), *Macro-Evolutionary Dynamics*, McGraw-Hill, New York.

Gal-Or, B. (1981), *Cosmology, Physics and Philosophy*, Springer Verlag, New York.

Gale, G. (1981), 'The Anthropic Principle', *Scientific American*, Vol. 245, pp. 154–171.

Goodall, J. (1963), 'My Life Among Wild Chimpanzees', *National Geographic Magazine.*, August, pp. 272–308.

Graves, R. (1960), *The Greek Myths*, Penguin Books.

Green, J.C. (1961), *The Death of Adam*, Mentor Books, New York.

Hall, B.G. (1991), 'Adaptive evolution that requires multiple spontaneous mutations: Mutations involving base substitutions', *Proceedings of the National Academy of Sciences, USA* Vol. 88, pp. 5882–5886.

Hauser, A. (1957), *The Social History of Art* (4 vols.), Random House, New York.

Hawking, S.T. (1988), *A Brief History of Time, From the Big Bang to Black Holes,* Bantam Books, New York.

Heisenberg, W. (1971), *Physics and Beyond,* Harper & Row Publications, New York.

Heisenberg, W. (1974), *Across the Frontiers,* Harper & Row Publications, New York.

Horgan, J. (1994), 'Can Science Explain Consciousness?', *Scientific American,* July, pp. 72–78.

Hofstadter, D.R. (1979), *Gödel, Escher, Bach: An Eternal Golden Braid,* Penguin Books.

Hussey E., (1972), *The Presocratics, Classical Life and Letters.* Gerald Duckworth & Co. Ltd.

Isaac, G.L (1983), 'Aspects of Human Evolution', in Bendall, D.S. (ed.), *Evolution from Molecules to Man,* Cambridge University Press, Cambridge.

Issar, A. (1979) 'Stratigraphy and paleoclimates of the Pleistocene of Central and Northern Israel', *Paleogeography, Paleoclimatology, Paleoecology,* Vol. 29, pp. 261–280,

Issar, A. (1980) 'A Space-Time Mind Continuum', *Speculations in Science and Technology,* Vol. 3, pp. 595–601.

Issar, A.S. (1982), 'Genesis, Observership, and Evolution in a Space-Time-Mind Continuum'. *Nature and System,* Vol. 4, pp. 13–22.

Issar,A. (1984), 'The Concept of 'Field' and the Contradiction between Necessity and Chance in Evolution', *Nature and System,* Vol. 6, No. 1, pp. 43–50

Issar, A. (1990), *Water Shall Flow from the Rock,* Springer Verlag. Heidelberg.

Keynes, J.M. (1962), *A Treatise on Probability,* Harper and Row Publishers, New York.

Kimura, M. (1983), *The Neutral Theory of Molecular Evolution,* Cambridge University Press.

King, L.W., (1951), *The Seven Books of Creation,* (Luzac and Co., London 1902), The University of Chicago Press.

Kramer, S.N. (1954), *History Begins at Sumer,* Doubleday Anchor Books, New York.

Kochav, S. and Eyal-Giladi, H. (1971), 'Bilateral Symmetry in Chick Embryo, Determination by Gravity', *Science,* Vol. 171, pp. 1027–1029.

Laplace, P., (1951 [1819]), *A Philosophical Essay on Probabilities,* Dover, New York.

Laurikainen, K.V. (1989), *Beyond the Atom, The Philosophical Thought of Wolfgang Pauli*, Springer Verlag, Berlin.

Leaky, L.S.B. (1960), *Adam's Ancestors, The Evolution of Man and His Culture*, Harper & Row Publications, New York.

Marshall, I.N. (1992), 'Towards a New Science of Consciuosness', *Proceedings of the International Symposium on Science and Consciousness*, Athens, 2–8 January,1992, organized by the Athenian Society of Science and Human Development, pp. 104–109.

Monod, J. (1972), *Chance and Necessity*, Vintage Books, New York.

Munitz, M.K. (1986), *Cosmic Understanding, Philosophy and Science of the Universe*, Princeton University Press, Princeton, N.J.

Murray, G. and Rogers, B.B. (1943), *Fifteen Greek Plays*. Oxford University Press, Oxford.

Pais, A. (1982), *Subtle is the Lord, The Science and Life of Albert Einstein*, Oxford University Press, Oxford.

Poincrè, H. (1952), *Science and Method*, Maitland, F. trans., Dover Publishing, New York.

Reichenbach, H. (1971), *The Direction of Time*, University of California Press.

Riedl, R. (1978), *Order in Living Organisms, A System Analysis of Evolution*, John Wiley and Sons.

Restak, R. (1991), *The Brain has a Mind of its Own: Insights from a Practicing Neurologist*. Harmony Books, Crown Publishers, New York.

Russell, B. (1937), *The Principles of Mathematics*, George Allen and Unwin Ltd., London.

Schrödinger, E. (1961), *My View of the World*, Cambridge Press, Cambridge.

Schrödinger, E. (1967), *What is Life — Mind and Matter*, Cambridge University Press, Cambridge.

Shannon, C.E. and Weaver, W. (1949), *The Mathematical Theory of Communication*, University of Illinois, Foundation of Classical Theory of Information, Urbana, IL.

Shallis, M. (1982), *On Time*, Penguin Books.

Shlain, Leonard (1991), *Art and Physics: Parallel Visions in Space, Time and Light*. William Morrow and Co., New York.

Simpson, G.G. (1983), *Fossils and the History of Life*, Scientific American Library, New York.

Snow, C.P. (1963), *The Two Cultures and a Second Look*. New American Library, New York, Toronto and London,

Stanley, M.S. (1981), *The New Evolutionary Timetable*, Basic Books, New York.

Stephens, M. (1988), *A History of News: From the Drum to the Satellite.* Penguin Books.
Thompson, Sir D'Arcy (1961), *On Growth and Form,* Bonner, J.T. (ed.), Cambridge University Press.
Tribus, M. (1961), *Thermodynamics: An Introduction to Energy, Information and States of Matter,* Van Norstrand, New York.
Von Bertalanfy, L. (1968), *General System Theory Foundations, Development, Applications,* George Braziller, New York.
Weiner, P. P. (1951), *Leibniz Selections.* Charles Scribners Sons, New York.
Weinberg, S. (1994), *Dreams of a Final Theory: The Scientist's Search for the Ultimate Laws of Nature.* Vintage, Random House, New York.
Wheeler, J.A. (1976), *Genesis and Observership,* John Henry Laboratories, Princeton University.
Whithrow, G.J. (1961), *The Natural Philosophy of Time,* Thomas Nelson & Sons, Ltd, London and Edinburgh.
Wilson, E.O. (1975), *Sociobiology: The New Synthesis,* Harvard University Press.
Zohar, D. (1991), *The Quantum Self,* Harper Collins, London.
Zohar, D. and Marshall, I.N. (1993), *The Quantum Society,* Bloomsbury, New York.